White Collar

Slacker's

Handbook

Tech Tricks to Fool Your Boss

Marc Saltzman

800 East 96th Street,
Indianapolis, Indiana 46240

WHITE COLLAR SLACKER'S HANDBOOK

International Standard Book Number: 0-7897-3310-2

Library of Congress Catalog Card Number: 2004099097

Printed in the United States of America

First Printing: April 2005

08   07   06   05   4   3   2   1

Trademarks

All terms mentioned in this book that are known to be trademarks or service marks have been appropriately capitalized. Que Publishing cannot attest to the accuracy of this information. Use of a term in this book should not be regarded as affecting the validity of any trademark or service mark.

Warning and Disclaimer

Every effort has been made to make this book as complete and as accurate as possible, but no warranty or fitness is implied. The information provided is on an "as is" basis. The author and the publisher shall have neither liability nor responsibility to any person or entity with respect to any loss or damages arising from the information contained in this book.

Bulk Sales

Que Publishing offers excellent discounts on this book when ordered in quantity for bulk purchases or special sales. For more information, please contact

U.S. Corporate and Government Sales
1-800-382-3419
corpsales@pearsontechgroup.com

For sales outside the United States, please contact

International Sales
international@pearsoned.com

Associate Publisher
Greg Wiegand

Acquisitions Editor
Todd Green

Development Editor
Laura Norman

Technical Editor
Greg Perry

Managing Editor
Charlotte Clapp

Project Editor
Mandie Frank

Copy Editor
Kezia Endsley

Indexer
Chris Barrick

Publishing Coordinator
Sharry Lee Gregory

Multimedia Developer
Dan Scherf

Designer
Anne Jones

Original Cartoon Artwork – cover and interior
Daryl Cagle

TABLE OF CONTENTS

About the Author

Marc Saltzman is a prolific freelance journalist, author, and radio and TV host who specializes in consumer electronics, computer software and hardware, video gaming, portable devices, and Internet trends.

Along with his weekly syndicated columns with Gannett News Service, USAToday.com, CNN.com, and the *National Post* (Canada), Marc currently contributes to more than 40 prominent publications, such as *USA Today, LA Times, AARP—The Magazine, The Costco Connection, Playboy,* Playboy.com, Microsoft @ Home, *Electronic Gaming Monthly, PC Gamer, Tribute, Feature, HUB,* and *Here's How.* Marc has authored 13 books and is a regular on-air technology expert on *Next @ CNN,* an award-winning tech show seen on CNN and its affiliates, and *MoneyWise,* seen on Global TV and the Prime Network in Canada.

Marc lives with his wife, Kellie, and three kids—twins Jacob and Maya, and Ethan—in Richmond Hill, Ontario, Canada.

Dedication

This book is dedicated to the world's overworked but underappreciated cubicle-dwelling white-collar slaves. Yes, that means you. Thanks for buying this book that teaches how to stick it to "the man." This book is also dedicated to my beautiful wife, Kellie, who is anything but a slacker thanks to our three kids—all of whom are still in diapers.

ACKNOWLEDGMENTS

A very special thank you goes out to everyone who helped me compile this ultimate high-tech slacking resource. This includes all the companies whose stellar products and services we've highlighted throughout these pages, all the ingenious websites covered, and each one of the interesting characters we've interviewed.

Thank you to Todd Green, acquisitions editor at Que Publishing, for his unwavering guidance, support, and professionalism. And although he was the closest thing to my "boss" on this book, I somehow didn't feel compelled to use many slacking techniques on him (okay, so a few slipped through undetected).

Thanks to Laura Norman, development editor at Que Publishing, for her direction and commitment to this fun project. A big thanks also goes to all the other folks at Que who had a hand in getting this project polished up and ready for you: Mandie Frank, Kezia Endsley, Charlotte Clapp, Chris Barrick, and Anne Jones.

Thank you to Daryl Cagle of Cagle Cartoons for the original artwork. You can see more of Daryl's work at www.caglecartoons.com or his professional cartoonist index at http://cagle.slate.msn.com.

WE WANT TO HEAR FROM YOU!

As the reader of this book, *you* are our most important critic and commentator. We value your opinion and want to know what we're doing right, what we could do better, what areas you'd like to see us publish in, and any other words of wisdom you're willing to pass our way.

As an associate publisher for Que Publishing, I welcome your comments. You can email or write me directly to let me know what you did or didn't like about this book—as well as what we can do to make our books better.

Please note that I cannot help you with technical problems related to the topic of this book. We do have a User Services group, however, where I will forward specific technical questions related to the book.

When you write, please be sure to include this book's title and author as well as your name, email address, and phone number. I will carefully review your comments and share them with the author and editors who worked on the book.

Email: feedback@quepublishing.com

Mail: Greg Wiegand
            Associate Publisher
            Que Publishing
            800 East 96th Street
            Indianapolis, IN 46240 USA

For more information about this book or another Que Publishing title, visit our Web site at www.quepublishing.com. Type the ISBN (excluding hyphens) or the title of a book in the Search field to find the page you're looking for.

Introduction

So, You Wanna Be a White Collar Slacker?

• • • • •

You're fed up, and for good reason.

Why is it that you're paid for a 40-hour work week but the last time you remember working only 9 to 5 you sang to your Wham! tape in the car on the way to the office (while using hairspray at a red light)?

Those days are over. And you can blame technology for that.

Personal computers, cell phones, and pagers, we were promised, would free up more personal time by helping us be more productive at work—yet they've done just the opposite.

A PC in your den now means you can take your work home with you. Great, so now you're analyzing sales reports, creating PowerPoint presentations, and answering email messages late at night, over weekends, and during holidays.

And forget about closing your eyes on that cross-country flight—that laptop ensures you'll be number crunching at 35,000 feet.

Even if you get into the office early to get a good start on the day, you find it takes the better part of 45 minutes just to wade through the spam in your inbox—especially when your boss won't spring for a better spam filter solution. Sigh.

That sleek new cell phone your boss so kindly gave to you really means he or she can reach you whenever and wherever. Yes, nothing like being called to chat about a troubled client while you're enjoying dinner at a fancy restaurant with your significant other.

Oh, and that sound you just heard was your kid scoring her first goal in soccer. Too bad your face was buried in your BlackBerry.

Ironically, these wireless devices have tethered us to the office more so than ever before.

Well, enough is enough.

Technology might have created a 24/7 work culture, but a handful of savvy white-collar cubicle dwellers are standing up to the "the man" and using these very same (de)vices—the PC, World Wide Web, email, and portable gadgets—to make it look like they're working when and where they're not.

White Collar Slacker's Handbook: Tech Tricks to Fool Your Boss teaches you how to slack off in a corporate world and not just get away with it but even make it look like you're a dedicated, tireless workaholic at the same time.

Okay, so this concept backfired for *Seinfeld*'s George Costanza, and the slackers who drag their heels in BBC's *The Office* didn't have the brains to pull this off effectively, but it can be done. Really.

This book helps you turn the tables so that you're not a slave to technology, but rather, you'll learn how to regain control over it.

For instance, in Chapter 1, "What, Didn't You Get My Email?" you will find out how to get more out of your email program. You'll set up a timer so that your note to the boss arrives in his inbox at 1 a.m. to make it look like you're burning the midnight oil when you really wrote it at 2 p.m. (before you skipped out early for the day). You'll learn how to forward your work email to another account so that you won't miss a note when you call in hung over—I mean, sick with a 24-hour flu—the following day. You'll discover how to manually change the clock on your PC so that it looks like you emailed something when you should have—although it was a day late.

In Chapter 2, "Chat Slack," instant messaging (IM) users can learn how to tweak the settings to make it appear they're diligently working away when they're really enjoying a three-martini lunch down the street.

Not allowed to spend time on the Web at the office? Chapter 3, "Remote Access Software, Your Best Friend," teaches how to log into your PC at home, remotely, so that you can surf to your heart's desire—without leaving a trail of where you've been online. Or on the flipside, learn how to remotely log into your office PC and pull up that day's newspaper to make it look like you've already been there—and you can do this from your car!

Instead of being leashed to your boss by a BlackBerry, wireless PDA, or SmartPhone, read Chapter 4, "Portable Gadgets Are Your Office away from the Office," to learn how to liberate yourself by making it look like you're at the office when you're really on the 10th hole of the golf course.

Gonna be late for work? Call the boss on your cell phone when you're still between the sheets, and set it up so she hears traffic noises in the background.

Chapter 5, "More Slacking Bites and Bytes," teaches about computer programs that allow you to make it sound like you're typing away when you're enjoying a short catnap or hide your game of solitaire by hitting a panic button. How about a screensaver that makes it look like you're installing a huge program (to buy you some time away from the desk)? You'll also arrange for an automated emergency phone call to your cell phone to get you out of a boring meeting.

Oh, and don't miss the humorous Chapter 6, "Office Shenanigans," with a handful of extra nuggets such as non-technical tips, terrific time-wasting websites, jokes to play on co-workers, and other clever tidbits.

This is just the beginning.

White Collar Slacker's Handbook: Tech Tricks to Fool Your Boss also features dozens of sneaky tips, tricks, and techniques for getting away with slacking off. And it's all spelled out in plain English, complete with step-by-step instructions and visuals to help you pull it off without a hitch.

Best of all, in learning how to abuse technology to slack off, this handbook in fact helps you learn more about your PC, its popular software, and your portable devices. How's that for irony?

Finally, don't feel like you need to read this cover to cover—simply flip to the pages that interest you the most. There are enough rules in the workplace—there are none here. Er, just make sure your boss doesn't see the title of this book!

Enjoy, happy slacking, and take a mental health day from time to time, will ya? You deserve it.

SLACKING WITH EMAIL...

- If you know you won't make it into work, forward your email to a handheld device or home-based email account—and reply as if you were at the office.

- Set up an email timer so your message to colleagues or your boss arrives at 2 a.m. when you wrote it at 11 a.m. Look at you burning the midnight oil! I smell a promotion.

- Change the time on your PC before sending an email to "prove" you emailed it when you said you did.

- If you don't want to face the music about something, reply with a doctored "automatic out-of-office reply" message.

...SO WHAT ARE YOU WAITING FOR, GET SLACKING!

Chapter 1
Hey, Didn't You Get My Email?

Email Timers, Forwards, Auto-Replies, and Other Sneaky Tricks

● ● ● ● ●

E mail. Could you live without it? Be honest. Probably not.

In just over a decade since its mainstream debut, electronic mail, or *email*, has become one of the most important communication tools for businesses everywhere.

In fact, according to IDC (www.idc.com), the number of person-to-person worldwide email messages sent on an average day in 2004 was 28.9 billion, or about 7.7 trillion annually. "Person-to-person" means these numbers do not include spammed messages or any other automated emails.

In the United States alone, typical email users receive an average of 198 messages per week in their primary personal and work email inboxes, totaling roughly 1.3 trillion per year. These incredible stats also do not account for blocked or filtered spam email. Wowza.

Yes, email has even trumped the ol' telephone, with all of its time-wasting small talk, wrong numbers, and that ever-so-annoying game of "voice mail tag."

If Marshall McLuhan was right—that the medium is the message—then how can you take advantage of this technology to give the impression you're working when you're not?

It's a lot easier to pull this off than you might think, even for technophobes whose VCR might still be blinking 12 o'clock.

So consider this chapter a discussion on how to use email to your advantage—how to impress the boss with your...ahem, tireless work ethic—when all you really want to do is play a round of golf, get a jump-start on pre-weekend traffic, or simply lie in bed to nurse a hangover.

Over the next few pages, you'll learn simple tricks and techniques on forwarding your email to a secondary account and how to make it look like you're replying to the email from the office. You'll also learn how to best use the "auto-reply" feature built into most email programs and much more.

Note...

We used Outlook 2003 and Outlook Express 6 for this book, as they are two of the more popular email programs for both home and work (and the latest version of each). If you are using older versions of this software, or other email programs altogether, it might take some exploration and experimentation to follow these tips. If you're stuck, be sure to refer to the program help file or the official website.

You'll also learn how to set an email timer with Microsoft Outlook so that you can have an email sent to your colleagues or boss at 1:34 a.m. to make it look like you're burning the midnight oil, when in fact you wrote the message at 3 p.m. before you left the office for the day!

ANSWER EMAIL FROM YOUR EASY CHAIR INSTEAD OF YOUR DESK CHAIR

- Forward email from your work account to a personal account, using either Outlook Express or Outlook 2003, and catch up on some much needed R&R.

- Reply to the forwarded emails without anyone knowing you're not really in the office today.

You know you won't make it into work tomorrow. Your favorite football team is in the playoffs, and not only did you score tickets to the game, you also caught wind of a party thrown afterward at an exclusive club where some of the players are said to be on the guest list. So, as a clever, forward-thinking individual, you fake a few coughs the day before, nonchalantly sniffle as you stroll pass your supervisor's office, and randomly hang your head in your hands at your cubicle. Before you leave for the day, you straighten up your desk and use your computer mouse to click off a little box that forwards all mail to your home account (after all, you don't want to miss anything important from your customers). Done and done.

If this scenario sounds appealing, read on.

Granted, many folks already know how to forward work-related email to another account for when you're out of the office, but it's a handy tool we shouldn't overlook in case you haven't set it up before.

Unless you've got the capability to remotely tap into your corporate email account from home or when traveling, the best way to see what's arriving in your inbox is to forward the email to a secondary account.

So much work... so little time

If you know your company's POP3 email settings, it's possible to have all corporate email picked up by a web-based email account such as Hotmail or Yahoo! Mail. Just be sure to close your email program at work so all new email will be picked up at home or on the road. Unless you've chosen to leave messages on the server, these emails picked up elsewhere won't be in your inbox at work—so keep this in mind! On the flip side, it's also possible to pick up your web-based email messages within Outlook or Outlook Express. That said, if you're using Hotmail, Gmail, or Yahoo! Mail to email résumés for another job, it's not a good idea to have that show up in your office email!

Some employees choose to have their email forwarded to their personal home accounts, whereas others set it up so messages go to a web-based email service such as MSN Hotmail (www.hotmail.com), Yahoo! Mail (mail.yahoo.com), or Google's Gmail (gmail.google.com).

The advantage to a web-based email account is that the basic service is completely free to use, and because it's a website service, email can be accessed by any Internet-connected computer, PDA, or cell phone anywhere in the world.

And now these web-based email services offer a lot more space than before. For example, Yahoo! Mail jumped from 4 megabytes (MB) of storage space to 250MB. Similarly MSN Hotmail, the world's most popular free web-based email service with more than 170 million users, went from 2MB of storage space to 250MB. Google's Gmail, the newest service out of the three, offers 1000MB (or 1 gigabyte) of storage space.

Setting up a free email account at one of these webmail sites is a breeze; simply choose an available email address (for example, ilovetoslackoff@hotmail.com or seeyouontheninthhole@yahoo.com), a password, and then give some information about yourself.

FORWARDING BASICS: THE STUFF YOU NEED TO KNOW

For both Outlook and Outlook Express, there are a few requirements for email forwards and auto-replies to work. These following points are for the work computer only—that is, the one that is forwarding the email to another PC altogether:

- You must have a constant connection to the Internet, such as a cable, DSL, T1, or T3 line. An Internet connection that uses a dial-up (telephone) modem will not work.

- Although your monitor doesn't need to be on, you must leave your computer on and Microsoft Outlook Express or Microsoft Outlook open.

Now it's time to edit your company's email account settings so that it'll automatically forward your incoming messages to this secondary account (unbeknownst to the sender). Of course, this assumes you are authorized to edit the email settings on your office computer!

LET OUTLOOK EXPRESS DO YOUR DIRTY WORK

If you are using Outlook Express 6, a free email program built into Microsoft's Internet Explorer browser (microsoft.com/ie), do the following:

1. Select Tools from the menu bar and then select Message Rules. Now, choose Mail from the list of options to open the Mail Rules window (see Figure 1.1).

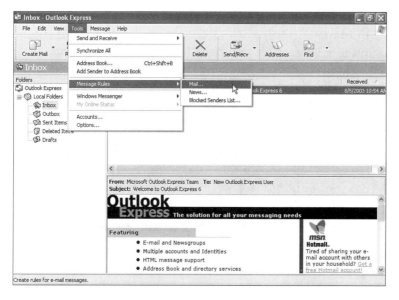

FIGURE 1.1

Outlook Express 6 users can easily set up an email forward to another account.

2. Now click New on the right side of the screen and a list of "conditions" pops up in Section 1.

Here you can specify the type of email to forward to another account. Options include the following:

- **For all messages**—Forwards email, regardless of who sent it.

- **Where the message has an attachment**—Useful if you're waiting on an important spreadsheet, document, or graphic, for example.

- **Where the message is from the specified account**—Forwards email from someone in particular.

You can scroll down to see all the available options—there's a ton of 'em.

Simply click your preference(s).

3. Section 2 asks you to select the "actions" for the rule you are creating. Use the mouse to check off your preferences, which will likely be Forward It To People. You have other choices, such as setting up an auto-reply to the sender (we'll get to this soon), so be sure to peruse these options.

4. The third area on this page (Section 3) will outline your rules thus far, but it is here where you need to specify the email address to send incoming messages to. Click the highlighted word People in the line Forward It To People and then type in the email address where you want messages sent (for example, donaldtrump@yourefired.com). See Figure 1.2 for help with completing this step.

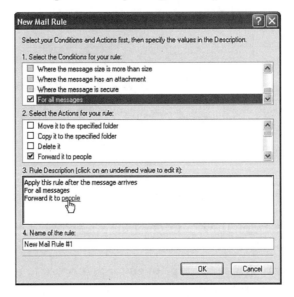

FIGURE 1.2
You can specify the rules for the incoming email messages here; clicking the word People under the rule description lets you select the email address(es) to which you want to forward messages.

5. The fourth and final section allows you to name this rule, such as "Forward to Home" or "Email Forwards to Yahoo!" or whatever. Click OK. That's it! Pretty easy, huh?

Going forward, anytime you want email forwarded to an alternate account, simply choose Tools, Message Rules and then check the box beside the rule you created to activate it (see Figure 1.3).

FIGURE 1.3
Easy as pie. Once you set it up, forwarding your email to an alternate account is just a couple mouse clicks away.

Remember, forwarding email does not delete it from your inbox at work— it simply makes a copy and forwards it to an alternate email address.

GET IN ON THE FUN WITH OUTLOOK 2003

Microsoft's Outlook (www.microsoft.com/outlook), which is bundled in the popular Microsoft Office system or can be purchased alone, is often referred to as the *de facto* mail program for businesses and homes alike.

Forwarding email in Outlook is more or less the same as with the Outlook Express freebie, albeit it a bit more difficult. Why? Because Outlook is a much more robust email program, so there are a wealth of additional options and

So much work... so little time

Want to know a fast way to launch an email message? In a web browser such as Internet Explorer, erase the "http://" in your Address window, type **mailto:** and then press Enter. This takes you right to Outlook or Outlook Express, with a message window open and ready for typing! Better yet, you can type the desired recipient's address in this space (for example, **mailto:rjones@ibm.com**) and the email will already be addressed to him. Neat, huh?

other bells and whistles to consider. But don't worry—it is actually a breeze to set up.

One issue to note before we get into the setup—if your Outlook program is used to pick up web-based email (http-based email), such as Hotmail or Yahoo! Mail, you will likely see a dialog box pop up on the screen with a message that warns these rules will not work on web-based mail accounts. Users may click where it says Do Not Show Me This Dialog again to prevent this warning from popping up in the future, but remember, these forwarding rules *will not work* for web mail accounts.

Trick the Boss

A good way to avoid staying late is to write a bunch of emails to co-workers or your boss and save them to your Drafts folder (clicking "Save" automatically puts them there). Then, at 4:55 p.m., open your Drafts folder and send them all at once—by the time the recipients open them and click to reply with a request (for example, "John, please create a chart with these figures ASAP"), you're out the door for the day! Bombardment isn't such a bad strategy, huh?!

Here's how to set up an email forward from your work account to another account:

1. In Microsoft Office Outlook 2003, select Tools from the menu bar and then select Rules and Alerts to open the Rules Wizard (see Figure 1.4). Now click New Rule.

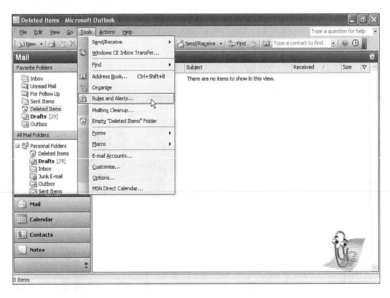

FIGURE 1.4
Setting up an email forward in Outlook is a little different than Outlook Express. This screen shows the first step. You with us so far?

2. Click the option at the top of the Rules Wizard dialog box to start from a Blank Rule.

3. Click Check Messages When They Arrive. Then click Next at the bottom of the Rules Wizard dialog box. This opens up a number of options, but for now we're only interested in forwarding all email messages that come in. That said, feel free to peruse all the options if you see something that sounds appealing to you.

4. Select the Through the Specified Account check box. In Step 2 of this page of the Rules Wizard, click the word Specified (highlighted in blue) to select the desired email account as shown in Figure 1.5.

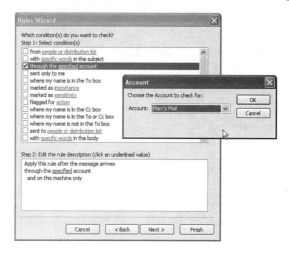

FIGURE 1.5
OK, so setting up an email forward in Outlook can be a tad tricky—but remember, you only need to do this once!

5. We're almost done—really. Once you've selected which email account to check for incoming messages, click Next.

6. Select the Forward It To People Or Distribution List check box. In the Step 2 area at the bottom of the Rules Wizard window, you will see the new rule added, but you must click the blue highlighted words People Or Distribution List to choose which email address to send it to (presumably your home or mobile account). This should open up your Outlook Contacts, where you can choose an email address to forward the messages to, but you can also type in a new email

address instead (toward the bottom, to the right of the word "to"). Click OK and you'll see the email address or distribution list name in the updated rules summary window, as shown in Figure 1.6.

Note...

Keep in mind that you can select more than one email address (for example, home and cell phone). You can also be more selective about what email messages to forward, such as those with a key word (such as "report," "assignment," or "important"), those with attachments, and so on. Have fun experimenting.

FIGURE 1.6
In this step you choose to which email address to send the message.

7. Before you finish up, you'll want to select any exceptions. For instance, you might prefer to only receive messages that are marked as important. Or, if you must log on to your remote account from a dial-up modem (for example, from a hotel that hasn't yet caught up to this century), you may choose *not* to forward messages with attachments, as it might take too long to download them. Simply click the box beside the desired exceptions, if any, and then select Next when you're finished.

8. The last step is to name your rule, such as "Forward to Home Account," and choose whether you want to activate this rule now or later. That's it!

All recent versions of Microsoft Outlook have an option under the Rules and Alerts settings to forward an email from someone in particular to your mobile device, such as a BlackBerry, cell phone, PDA, or SmartPhone. Figure 1.7 shows the options to select to set this up.

FIGURE 1.7
Depending on your email program, an option might exist to immediately forward a specific message to a handheld device as it comes in.

TRICKS AND OTHER SNEAKY STUFF TO DO WHEN REPLYING TO FORWARDED MAIL

Once you've forwarded your email to a secondary account at home or on the Web, you can reply to it. There are some tricks you can pull off to make it look like the replies were sent from the office. It's not foolproof, but at a casual glance from the recipient, the emails won't look suspicious. And hey, even if your customers or colleagues realize you're writing back from a web-based email account, it looks like you're diligently working from home or on the road, anyway!

First of all, the subject line in the email (for example, "sales report deadline") will have a "fw:" in

Don't Get Caught
If you know you can't possibly get that important email in by Friday morning as requested by your boss, ask whether Saturday morning will do. The good news here is that no boss in her right mind is at the PC on the weekend checking for email, so that Saturday a.m. message can really be sent by Monday morning—as long as it's before the boss gets to the office!

front of it, indicating the message was forwarded to another email account. When you click Reply and fill in the recipient's email address, be sure to manually replace the "fw:" with a "re:" as though you were merely responding to the original email.

Now you'll want to enter the email Settings (or Customization or Preferences depending on your email application) area of your secondary email account so that the recipient believes the email was sent from work, and not from a home or a web-based email account.

Here's how to do it:

1. When logged into your web-based email account, such as Yahoo! Mail (mail.yahoo.com), click on the Mail Options tab in the upper right-hand corner of the screen, by your email address (for example, johnsmith@yahoo.com).

2. Once inside, click the Mail Accounts section. Now you will see your name or the default setting, which is simply Yahoo! Mail. Click Edit. Here, you can change the name that should appear on the From line of all outgoing mail, and more importantly for our purposes, it's possible to change the Reply To account. This is where you type in your corporate email address (for example, name@company.com), so it'll be displayed instead of the Yahoo! address (see Figure 1.8).

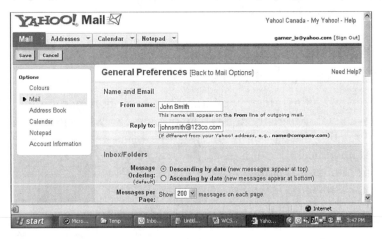

FIGURE 1.8

If you don't want someone to know you're not in the office, edit the Preferences/Options section of your web-based email service (such as Yahoo! Mail, pictured here) and change the Reply To field to your company info.

Reproduced with permission of Yahoo! Inc. © 2005 by Yahoo! Inc. YAHOO! and the YAHOO! logo are trademarks of Yahoo! Inc.

FAKE A CORRUPTED DOCUMENT

Here's a trick to try when you're really in a bind. Say you were supposed to email a Word document with some information to your boss. You haven't finished this assignment yet, so what can you do? It's devious, but you can create a "fake" Word document that will have nothing inside of it but gobbledygook—that is, all kinds of numbers, letters, and strange symbols. When he opens the document and sees this, it'll look like the file is corrupt. Play dumb and say, "Really? That's strange. Lemme send it again." Hopefully this will be a day or two later, so make sure you have the *real* file this time! How to create this document, you ask? Go to Windows Explorer or My Computer and take any file—such as a screensaver or picture file (nothing over 1MB in size) and rename the file with ".doc" as the new extension. Windows will warn you: "If you change a file extension, it may become unusable." Click Yes. Now double-click the file and you'll see that crazy text inside! Be sure, however, to make a backup of the original file (for example, a digital photo) or you might not be able to get it back. See Figure 1.9 for an example of what this faux document could look like. Sneaky, but it could buy you some time!

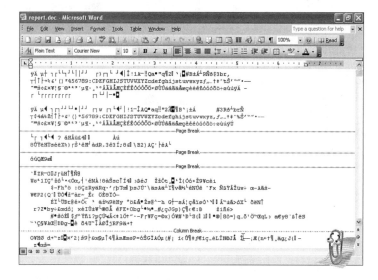

FIGURE 1.9
You're not going to get away with this too often, so use it sparingly...

EMAIL AUTO-REPLIES—IT'S LIKE HAVING YOUR OWN PERSONAL ASSISTANT

- Okay, setting this feature up in Outlook Express does involve that "r" word (Rules), but it's really a breeze.

- For Outlook 2003 users this is a bit more tricky, but once it's done, you won't have to do it again.

When you're out of the office and you want to look like you're a hard-working, responsible employee to your boss, co-workers, clients, or customers, you may choose to set up an automated reply in your email program. These are also referred to as "out of office" auto-replies.

Typically, they say something like this:

> Thank you for your email. I'm currently out of the office with limited access to email. I will be back on Thursday, April 5, but if this matter is urgent, please feel free to call me on my mobile phone at XXX-XXX-XXXX.

Many folks set their email program to reply with this message to all senders, or from a specific

So much work... so little time

Many seasoned users of Microsoft Outlook or Outlook Express are aware of the "read receipt" feature, which asks the recipient to let the sender know the message has arrived. However, there are times when you don't want the recipient to know that you are interested in knowing whether the message was read. Introducing DidTheyReadIt (www.didtheyreadit.com)—a clever program that not only tells you whether someone has read your email, but also what day and time it was read, for how long, and what city they were in! And of course, the recipient has no idea you're getting this important information. After all, haven't you ever sent an important email to a co-worker who didn't follow-up or do what you asked, and then said "Oh, I didn't see that email." Well, now you can find out for sure. Users can try DidTheyReadIt for free for 10 email messages, but then must cough up $25 for three months, or $50 for a year.

account. Not that we'd encourage you to take advantage of this handy technological tool, but it does buy you some time if someone is expecting something from you! For example, say lazy Larry is falling behind in the shipment of some products to an important customer. Setting up this auto-reply lets the customer know he likely won't get in touch with Larry until Thursday. Don't abuse this feature, however, as some might think "Gee, Larry is never in the office!"

The next couple of sections show you how to set up an email auto-reply using Outlook Express or Microsoft Outlook 2003.

So much work... so little time

If you want to impress your boss and co-workers, search the Internet for intelligent-sounding quotations (such as those from www.bartleby.com) and add one to your signature file that appears at the end of all your email messages. You can add desired text by clicking on the Tools tab, then Options, Mail Format. In the "Compose In This Message Format" list, click the message format that you want to use the signature with. Then, under Signatures, select an email account, and then choose the signatures that you want to use for new messages, replies, and forwards. Some programs, such as IncrediMail (www.incredimail. com), let you use your own hand-written signature to appear at the end of the email message. However, this could pose a security threat, so it's not recommended!

TOOLS AND RULES: SETTING UP AUTO-REPLIES WITH OUTLOOK EXPRESS

In Outlook Express, click the Tools menu and then select Message Rules, Mail.

Here you have one of two options: You can add an email auto-reply to an existing rule (such as forwarding the email to a secondary account), or create a new rule altogether. If you want to add an auto-reply to an existing rule, highlight the rule and then click Modify. Otherwise, click New. The rest of these instructions are the same whether you're creating a new rule or modifying an existing one.

1. In the top box under Select the Conditions for Your Rule, select For All Messages if this option works for you. (You might have to scroll down in the box to locate this option—it's at the bottom.) Other options are available here as well, such as replying only to messages that have an attachment.

2. In the second (middle) box, under Select the Actions for Your Rule, click the box that says Reply with Message as shown in Figure 1.10. (Again, scroll down the list of rule options until you see the right one.)

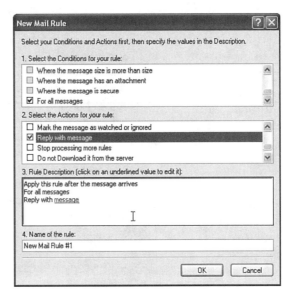

FIGURE 1.10
Easy stuff. Here we're setting up an email auto-reply so senders will know you're out of the office—you know, for when you're at home watching HBO.

3. Now you'll need to write the email message that the sender will receive. Click the word Message highlighted in blue at the bottom under Rule Description. The Open dialog box appears for you to select the auto-reply message file stored on your computer.

Don't Get Caught

If you don't want to deal with an email request from a client or customer, you can fake an "out of office" auto-reply. Simply click Reply and change the subject line, change it to something like "Out of Office Auto Reply." and inside the message, just type one line: "*[Your name]* is out of the office until July 27." It might just buy you some time!

Here's the tricky part. You could create an email document containing your automated reply and save it as an .eml message (the .eml extension indicates an Outlook Express email file), but your best bet is to create a text document instead. Why, you ask? It is often preferred because an .eml message may only be *attached* to the auto-reply instead of being sent as the text inside the email message itself (depending on the recipient's email program and/or settings). Recipients might not want to click attachments for obvious reasons, such as a potential virus, or it might be filtered out altogether by their email provider.

To create a text message, here's what to do:

1. Leave your Outlook Express Rules Wizard as is for the moment. On the Windows Task bar, click Start and then select All Programs (or Program Files). Now select Accessories and then Notepad.

2. Type your message and then save this file somewhere on your computer—but remember where you saved it (the Windows Desktop is likely the easiest)! See Figure 1.11 for an example.

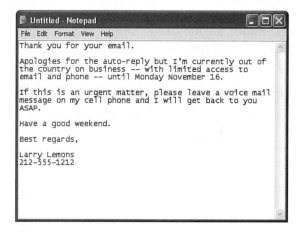

FIGURE 1.11

Here is an example of a decent auto-reply message. Keep it for future reference, but remember to change the particulars, such as the return date, and so forth.

3. Now go back to the Outlook Express Rules Wizard and select your text message file as the auto-reply file. You will need to click the Files of Type pull-down menu near the bottom of the dialog box and

change it from Mail (*.eml) to Text (*.txt). You can use the Look In drop-down list at the top of the Open dialog in order to find the text file on your hard drive (see Figure 1.12).

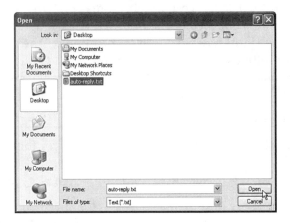

FIGURE 1.12
Find the newly created auto-reply text file on your computer and attach it to these rules.

4. Once you highlight the file (for example, auto-reply.txt), click Open and a confirmation of the chosen file appears in the Rule Description window of the Rules Wizard (see Figure 1.13).

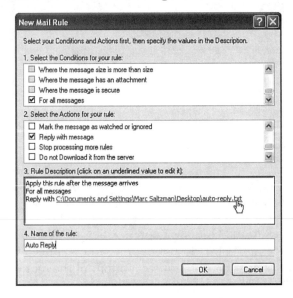

FIGURE 1.13
The last step is to name this rule, such as "Auto Reply" or "Out of Office Message"—as seen here at the bottom of the screen.

5. If it looks good, name this rule (for example, Auto Reply) and then click OK.

When you need to use this auto-reply feature in the future, simply select the Tools, Rules in Outlook Express and click the rule to invoke it.

Now send yourself a test email to check whether it's working!

HAVING A SLACK ATTACK? SET UP YOUR AUTO-REPLIES IN OUTLOOK 2003

Unless you're using a Microsoft Exchange Server email account (see note), setting up an email auto-reply in Microsoft Outlook is a bit more cumbersome. But remember, you only need to do this once.

Note...

If you are using a Microsoft Exchange Server email account, this process is a lot easier. Click the Tools menu and then select Out of Office Assistant. Now select I Am Currently out of the Office. Here you can type the message you want to send to others while you're out of the office. This message will only be shown to the sender once.

1. In Microsoft Outlook, select Tools from the menu bar, and then select Options, Mail Format.

2. Uncheck the box that says Use Microsoft Word As Your Email Editor or something similar. Click OK to close this window.

3. Click the New Message button on the shortcuts bar to start a new email and type your desired auto-reply. You do not need to address this message to anyone, but put something in the Subject line that senders will recognize in their email inbox.

Don't Get Caught

If you're forwarding an email message to your boss, be sure that the message string (the history of messages and replies, beginning from the first email) does not contain anything inappropriate. This text is usually buried down inside the email. Employees have been fired by trashing the boss in an email with a co-worker, only to forward the email message on to the boss, unaware of previous comments inside the message! You can manually delete this history before forwarding, or you can choose not to include past messages inside of an email reply in the Outlook options.

4. When completed, select File, Save As and use the Save As Type pull-down menu to select Outlook Template (*.oft). The default save folder will be Templates, which is fine, but be sure to name this template accordingly, such as "Email Auto Reply.oft" (see Figure 1.14).

FIGURE 1.14
Type your "out of office" email reply and save it as an Outlook Template for future reference.

5. Click Save and you can close this email, even if it warns that you haven't saved it.

Note...

If you use Word as your email editor, be sure to re-activate it before you forget! Follow the instructions in steps 1 and 2 again to check the box that tells Outlook to use Word as your email editor.

Now it's time to edit the rules. In Outlook, select Tools, Rules and Alerts, New Rule. Alternatively, you can select Change Rule and then Edit Rule Settings to add an email auto-reply to an existing rule. Yes, let's do that—we'll add the "auto-reply" rule to the existing "forward mail" rule. After all, when you're out of the office, you'll want the sender to know you're away *and* you'll want that message forwarded to you elsewhere, no?

1. If the conditions are fine (that is, these rules will apply to all senders), click Next to add this extra action.

   Remember, if you don't want your mail sent to another account, create an all new "auto-reply" rule and follow these same instructions instead of editing the "forwarding" rule.

2. Now click Reply Using a Specific Template and select your newly created email auto-reply (see Figure 1.15).

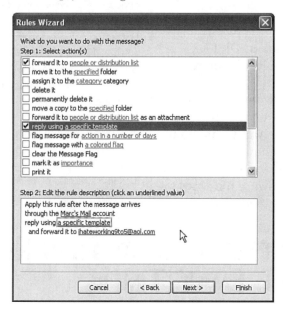

FIGURE 1.15
In Outlook, users can set up an auto-reply message by checking the box that says Reply Using a Specific Template and selecting the appropriate one.

3. Clicking the words A Specific Template in the Edit the Rule Description window prompts a new window. From the pull-down menu, select User Templates in File System and you'll see your new template in this directory. Double-click it and you'll see that it's been added to your rule description. Click Next.

4. If there are exceptions you want to add to this rule, you can check them off here. If there are no exceptions to this rule, click Next again

and then click Finish. Feel free to rename this rule. You may also activate it now—it's a good idea to test it first.

You can now turn this rule on or off at any time in Outlook by selecting Tools, Rules and Alerts and checking the box beside the rule.

Food for thought: In case you don't use Outlook or Outlook Express, or if you prefer more robust options, there are a handful of third-party auto-reply programs available on the Internet. Type in a few keywords into your favorite search engine, such as Google (www.google.com), or visit a shareware/freeware file repository such as Download.com.

So much work... so little time

Have you ever tried to cut and paste text from a website into an email and you get all these funky formatting issues: some words are bigger than others, a different color, or there's a huge space between some paragraphs? Well, there are two quick ways to get around this. The first is to cut the text from the website, and when you paste it into a Word document or email, select "Paste Special" instead of the regular "Paste" (located under the Edit tab). This will paste the text with no weird formatting nonsense! A second way is to simply cut and paste the desired text into Notepad (in Windows XP, go to Start, All Programs, Accessories). Then cut and paste the text into your email, and the words will look like a regular ol' email that you typed up.

IT IS BETTER TO SEND THAN RECEIVE: FUN WITH EMAIL TIMERS

Ah, setting an email timer is one of my favorite tricks for making your boss or colleagues believe you're hard at work while they're enjoying their beauty rest. Ahem.

The idea is that you can write an email message at, say, 2 p.m., but you've configured Microsoft Outlook (sorry, Outlook Express users) to send the email at 1:31 a.m. What praise you'll receive from the boss for your tireless work ethic! This trick also works for

Trick the Boss

Here's another way to "fake time" using your favorite email program. Let's say you were supposed to submit a report to your boss by 4 p.m. If it's after 5 p.m., you can set the clock on your PC back a few hours and then send the email. (Don't forget to change it back again right away so you don't forget to do it later!) It will still arrive late in your boss's inbox, but the Sent time will say 1:30 p.m., supporting your argument that you indeed sent her what she was looking for after lunch, and you don't know why it took so long to get there.

making it look like you're staying late at the office (for example, 7:21 p.m.) or holidays and weekends, of course.

The following steps show you how to set up this diabolical scheme.

1. Step 1 is simple enough: Write your email message. You can refer to the fact that it's quite late/early if you want (in case she doesn't read the time it was emailed). Perhaps you could write something like this:

"Well it took me more than four hours to crunch these numbers (finished at 1:15 a.m.!) but wanted you to have this when you got into the office."

OK, so that's a bit much for those who don't like to kiss butt, but you get the idea. See Figure 1.16 for another example.

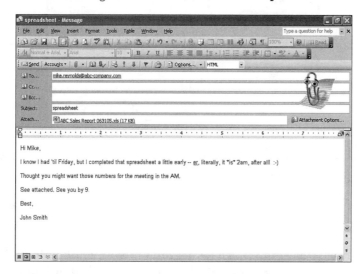

FIGURE 1.16
OK, so it's lying. We know.

3. When you're finished writing your message, click the Options button in the upper-middle portion of the Outlook window, and from the list of delivery options, click the box beside the words Do Not Deliver Before. Refer to Figure 1.17 to see how you can select the date and time when this message should be delivered using the drop-down boxes for those fields.

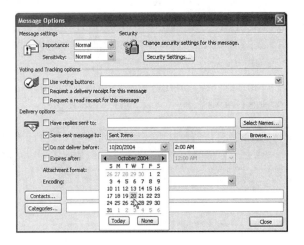

FIGURE 1.17
What a cinch—here's how to set up a timer for a given email message within Microsoft Outlook.

4. Once a date and time is chosen, the last step is to click Close and then click Send.

You should see this email message pending in your Outbox folder! You will need to keep Outlook open for this email to be sent at 2 a.m. Oooh, look how sneaky you are. Don't worry—this is our dirty little secret.

SLACKING WITH INSTANT MESSAGING

- Fix your IM software so you can step out for that three-hour lunch and no one can keep tabs on you.

- Log into your office IM program before you leave home so it looks like you're already in the office!

- Edit existing "away" messages (or create new ones) so no one knows the real reason you've not answered your IM messages all morning is that you're on the back nine of your favorite golf course.

- Tweak your IM settings to make it look like you're at an important offsite meeting.

- Got a cell phone with text messaging capability (who doesn't these days)? Stay on the move without missing a single IM.

...SO WHAT ARE YOU WAITING FOR, GET SLACKING!

Chapter 2
Chat Slack

Using Instant Messaging Programs to Trick Your Boss

• • • • •

E mail might still be the most popular way to communicate among computer users, but there are many other PC tools to impress the boss with your, ahem, tireless work ethic—when all you really want to do is slack off.

Ever thought of using—or abusing—your favorite instant messaging program to fake your enormous workload? Oh, but there is so much you can do. Read on.

Instant messaging—the wildly popular Internet chatting tool—has now climbed to a whopping 63 million users in the U.S. and is estimated to be used by a quarter billion Net surfers worldwide. It has become so ubiquitous, in such a short amount of time, that the adoption rate of instant messaging (IM) services continues to outpace that of the Internet itself, with a total time spent using IM services up 48 percent at home and 110 percent at work from just a couple of years ago.

Note...

Didya Know? America Online owns three instant messaging services: AOL IM (as part of the AOL service), AIM (which stands for America Online Instant Messenger, available to everyone), and an incredibly popular service outside of North America, ICQ.

For the uninitiated, instant messaging programs let users chat in real time, opposed to the back-and-forth method found in turn-based email. What's more, IM programs allow you to chat with multiple people at once (even with a microphone or video webcam!), play multiplayer games, swap files such as photos and music, or even collaborate on documents, spreadsheets, presentations, and other files—in real time—all the while chatting throughout the process. See Figure 2.1 for an example of a file being sent via Yahoo! Messenger.

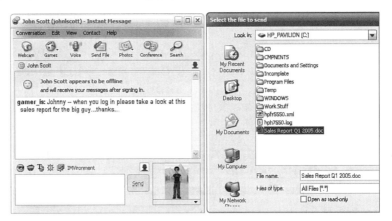

FIGURE 2.1
To save time and increase productivity, IM users can swap documents and even work on them together in real time. Pictured here is Yahoo! Messenger.
Reproduced with permission of Yahoo! Inc. © 2005 by Yahoo! Inc. YAHOO! and the YAHOO! logo are trademarks of Yahoo! Inc.

Other IMs, such as MSN Messenger, include a handy whiteboard feature so you can start from a clean slate and draft up the next million-dollar idea. The whiteboard is under the Tools tab. What's more, many search functions are now embedded into IM programs. In the chat window of Yahoo! Messenger, type **s:** and then what you're searching for (for example, "music stores Chicago"). The info and web links will pop up immediately. See Figure 2.2 for an example.

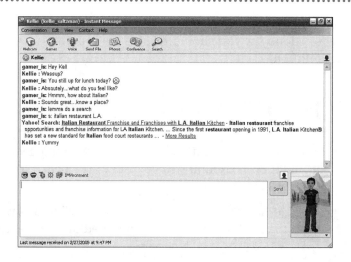

FIGURE 2.2

An example of two co-workers planning lunch via IM. Typing "s: Italian restaurant L.A." takes advantage of Yahoo! Messenger's integrated search functionality.

Reproduced with permission of Yahoo! Inc. © 2005 by Yahoo! Inc. YAHOO! and the YAHOO! logo are trademarks of Yahoo! Inc.

This chapter offers a handful of tips on how to use your favorite IM program to become a white-collar slacker superhero.

We'll include step-by-step instructions for three of the most popular IM services in North America: **AOL's AIM** (www.aim.com), **MSN Messenger** (http://messenger.msn.com/), and **Yahoo! Messenger** (http://messenger.yahoo.com/). In writing this chapter, we used the latest versions of each IM program at the time, but remember that you might have an older or newer version, so the walkthrough portions might require a bit of tweaking on your part.

Don't Get Caught

Want to look good in your boss's eyes? Before you leave home for the office each morning, go to your computer and log into your IM. This way, even if the boss comes in early to work and logs on, he or she will see that you're already online—and the first one in the "office" to boot. Remember: IM buddy lists are the 21st century "punch clock" because you can see when people log on and off! You can pull this off in one of two ways. One is to download the same IM program (also referred to as an IM client) at home as the one at the office and use the same screen name to log in. Another way is to use the web-based version of your IM if it has one, such as AIM Express (www.aim.com/get_aim/express) and log on using your work identity.

One last thing—if you're unsure about how these changes will affect your IM's look or functionality, you should refer to the program's help files or other documentation.

DISABLING THE IDLE NOTIFICATION

- Learn how to make it look like you're working away on your office PC even though you've been at the beach for the past three hours.

- Find out how to creatively alter your "idle" and "away" messages to give the impression you're tied up in meetings.

- Make your IM program active when Windows starts so your boss thinks you've been working longer than you have been.

Slackers beware: Most instant messaging programs will let others know when you've been away from your PC. What's this? You didn't know that your supervisor or boss was aware when you took that 20-minute coffee break with Joe from accounting? If your boss is on the list of people in your IM community (often referred to as a buddy list), he or she can see whether you've been active. Let's face it—that dirty little four-letter word—*idle*—does have a negative connotation, no?

Fret not—follow these simple rules to turn off the notification that reveals to others when you haven't been at your desk in ages. Whose business is it anyway, right? Little do they know you're dealing with some bad Mexican food you ate the night before. Also, keep in mind, you might be yanked into a last-minute meeting and don't have time to log out of your IM program—you don't want your offsite customers or clients to think you're slacking off, right? And when you're yanked into one of those last-minute meetings and don't have time to log out of your IM program your offsite customers or clients won't think you're slacking off, right?

Because instant messaging programs are the new office "punch clocks," some savvy users elect to have their IM log in whenever they boot up their PC. Otherwise, if you forget to log into your IM manually, your boss (or that co-worker who thinks he's your boss...you know the one) might not be aware you've arrived at the office. Setting this up is a breeze. For instance, with AIM, click Setup, and then Preferences, and then the Sign On/Off option on the left side. Here you can click Start AIM when Windows Starts (see Figure 2.3).

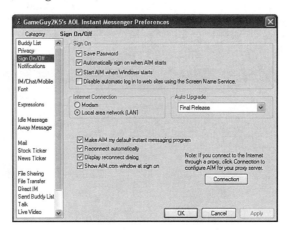

FIGURE 2.3
Click the Start AIM when Windows Starts option to select it—otherwise you might forget to do so and it'll look like you're not at your desk at 9 a.m. when you really were. Er, on that note, don't select this option if you're chronically late!

Note...

Many AIM users have grown accustomed to using AIM Bots—these optional Buddy List "robots" let users chat with AI-driven characters that can help you in some way. For example, AOLBuddy provides weather, movie times, games, and more, whereas ZolaOnAOL can define words, offer a calculator, and give news or horoscope information right inside the IM window. Find out more about AIM Bots at www.aim.com, and then click IM Robots along the left side of the page. Hmm, too bad there isn't a 'bot smart enough to carry a business conversation for you while you're on the golf course.

AIM USERS

If you are an AIM user, follow these steps to disable the idle notification:

1. From your Buddy List window, click Setup near the bottom right.

2. Click Preferences.

3. On the left side of the screen, click Privacy.

4. Half-way down the page you'll find a check box labeled Allow users to see how long I've been idle. Be sure this box is unchecked!

5. Once completed, click OK or Apply (see Figure 2.4).

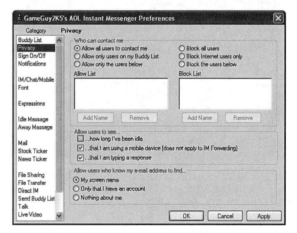

FIGURE 2.4
Don't let your AIM buddies know how long you've been away from your PC! They're nosy enough, no?

YAHOO! MESSENGER USERS

To disable the idle notification in Yahoo! Messenger, follow these simple steps:

1. Double-click the Yahoo! Messenger icon in your system tray (the little smiley face near the clock on your PC) to launch the IM client.

2. From the main window, click the Messenger tab at the top of the screen.

3. Click Privacy Options.

4. Under Idle Status, click the box that has the label Do not show anyone how long I have been idle.

5. Click OK or Apply (see Figure 2.5).

FIGURE 2.5

It's a cinch to disable this tell-all idle message that's built into the Yahoo! Messenger software.

Reproduced with permission of Yahoo! Inc. © 2005 by Yahoo! Inc. YAHOO! and the YAHOO! logo are trademarks of Yahoo! Inc.

That's all there is to it!

MSN MESSENGER USERS

This one is slightly different, but still pretty easy to fix:

1. Launch MSN Messenger and click the Tools tab at the top of the window.

2. Click Options from the pull-down menu.

3. Under the area titled My Status, you can uncheck the rule that says Show me as "Away" when I'm inactive for 5 minutes. Or you can increase that number to 60 minutes if you'd like to keep the idle notification but don't want it to kick in immediately.

4. Click OK (see Figure 2.6).

Don't Get Caught

If you're supposed to be working but instead decide to go to a friend's house to lounge, head over to any Internet-connected PC there and log onto your IM using your work identity. Turn up the volume on the computer's speakers and resume your DVD movie or cocktails on the back porch or whatever. When you hear a "ping" that tells you a colleague or client has sent you a message, saunter back over to the computer and respond. For all they know, you're somewhere in the office, right?

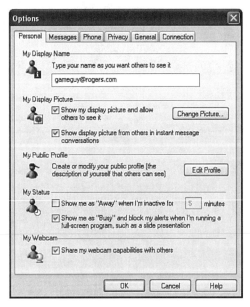

FIGURE 2.6
The My Status area is where you can disable the "I've been away from my PC far too long and happily getting away with it" notification!

EDITING THE AWAY OR BUSY MESSAGES

- Create unique IM auto-responses to fool—or impress—your boss.

- Find out how to create custom IM "rules" that you can easily toggle on and off as you step away from your desk.

- Forward your IM to your cell phone so your vacationing boss won't know that you're not at your desk!

- Discover how to keep a record of all your IM chat logs in case you need them in the future.

Even though you deserve a lunch break, it doesn't look good to your customers, clients, or colleagues if they try to send you an IM and it's unanswered, or if an auto-response says you're away from your desk.

If you want to look professional, you can create custom auto-responses for when you're away from your PC. After all, if you're on the golf course with your old high-school buddy who just drifted into town, wouldn't it be more impressive to your IM sender if the response read: "I'm in a three-hour offsite meeting. If this is urgent, please call my cell phone"? 'Nuff said.

Instead of an auto-response, some IM programs let you have a short message attached to your name as it appears on the messenger list (for example, Yahoo! Messenger). Same idea, but a different way to make others think you're busy turning the company into a Fortune 500 enterprise!

AIM USERS

If you use AIM, here's the way to change your auto-response message:

1. From your AIM window, click the Away tab (near the bottom beside Setup) as shown in Figure 2.7. A list of options will pop up.

FIGURE 2.7
Click the Away button (near the bottom right of this AIM window) and select the desired action.

2. Click Edit Away Messages (the second option from the top). As you can see, the default Away Message text is simply: "I am away from my computer right now." Surely you can come up with a better message than that.

3. Click Default Away Message under the Labels for messages area, and then click the Edit button and start typing your response.

4. When you're done, click Save.

Alternatively, you can make a new label name for this rule before typing in the auto-reply message. Simply click the Add Message button, type a name for your new label, and type your new custom message (See Figure 2.8).

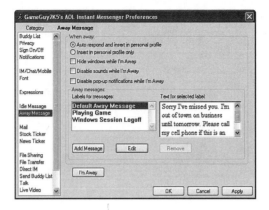

FIGURE 2.8
You can also create a custom Idle message here to appear when you're away from the PC for a short length of time. The left window (in the middle of the screen) is where you can add a label for a custom message you might want to use in the future.

YAHOO! MESSENGER USERS

Here's how to change the status beside your name in your messenger list (a.k.a. Friends list). This way, you can create a custom description that's different than the default ones that ship with this IM client ("Be Right Back" or "On the Phone").

1. Click on your name or picture at the top of the IM window and then select the desired option from the pull-down menu that appears (see Figure 2.9).

2. Click New Status Message. (Alternatively, you can click Messenger at the top and then click Change My Status.)

So much work... so little time

If you're trying to get work done but your friends and co-workers are nagging you via IM, you can choose to become "invisible" so it'll appear as if you're offline. The good news is that you can still see who's online and even send a message! It's easy to set this up. In AIM, click on the little eyeball beside your name and it'll close the eye. Now you're invisible! Click it again to become visible. In Yahoo! Messenger, click your name beside your avatar and, from the pull-down menu, choose Invisible to Everyone. If you want to be invisible only to certain people in your messenger list, right-click on someone's name and select Stealth Settings before choosing your option. In MSN Messenger, click your name and select the option that says Appear Offline.

FIGURE 2.9
It's not rocket science (really). Inside the Yahoo! Messenger window, click your screen name at the top (here it's gamer_is). Then click New Status Message and begin typing your status.

Reproduced with permission of Yahoo! Inc. © 2005 by Yahoo! Inc. YAHOO! and the YAHOO! logo are trademarks of Yahoo! Inc.

3. Enter the text for your new status message (such as "Out of town at a conference until Friday").

4. Click OK.

Now, when you access the pull-down menu by clicking on your name, you'll see your new status message as an option (see Figure 2.10).

FIGURE 2.10
Now you can start a collection of interesting status messages and they'll all be stored here. Just click your name and a pull-down menu with default and custom status blurbs can be accessed when needed. Be creative!

Reproduced with permission of Yahoo! Inc. © 2005 by Yahoo! Inc. YAHOO! and the YAHOO! logo are trademarks of Yahoo! Inc.

FORWARDING YOUR MESSAGES TO A MOBILE PHONE

- Forward your IM chats to your cell phone (while you're still in bed) so you won't miss a beat.

- With the aid of a video camera and your favorite IM, find out how to fake being in one location when you're in another.

- Discover the awesome solo or multiplayer games offered by your favorite IM program.

Ah, now this one is golden. Say you're not in the office. And you should be. By toying with the settings of your favorite instant messaging program, you can have all IMs sent to your cell phone. No kidding. Then you can reply as if you were in front of your PC like a diligent little worker. No one will know you're really sipping delicious Cosmopolitans with your unemployed friend, Stu. Er, just be sure your response is legible!

AIM USERS

Open AIM and near the bottom of the window, click the tab that says Away (or you can click My AIM at the top of the window and select Away Message). Now select Forward to Mobile. If it's the first time you've clicked it, a web page will pop up and ask you to verify your IM password for security reasons

So much work... so little time

If you're the type of person who likes to keep a record of everything—you know, just in case—then consider the option in some IM programs to automatically archive all conversations in a folder on your hard drive for future reference. Perhaps your co-worker will attempt to get out of a project that he agreed to accept via IM a while back (and tries to dump on your shoulders!). In MSN Messenger, for example, from the main menu, click Tools, and then Options, and then Messages. Look for the Message History area near the middle of the page. Click the box where it says Automatically keep a record of my conversations. You can also select where to save these documents. In Yahoo! Messenger, click Preferences (under the Messenger tab) and then select Archive on the left side to peruse your options. Cool, huh?

(see Figure 2.11). After this is completed, you will be asked to register your phone number. As long as you have a text messaging option on your cell phone (and chances are you do), you're in luck.

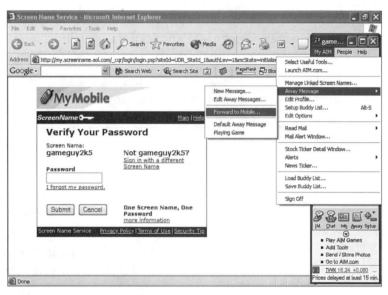

FIGURE 2.11
Setting up AIM to forward messages to your cell phone.

After you've set this up, to activate IM forwarding to your cell phone, click Setup, and then Preferences. Choose IM/Chat/Mobile on the left side. Now click the tab that says Forward IMs to your mobile phone.

If someone sends you a message, they will see a response that says something like this: "Your IM has been sent to my mobile device. When I receive it, I will be able to reply. Thanks for your IM!" What's more, you can choose whether you want your contacts to see that you're using a mobile phone. In the Setup area, under Privacy tab, you can select or deselect the option that says Allow users to see that I am using a mobile device. Sweet. If your buddies have selected this mobile phone option, a little cell phone will appear by their names in the Buddy List. While these IM-to-mobile phone-forwarding services are free, they might result in more airtime with your phone carrier, so it could cost you more there.

Some phones now come pre-installed with an AIM client. This way, you can log on and engage in instant messaging via your AIM account even though you're sitting near third base at a Red Sox game (with company seasons tickets, no less)! Also keep in mind that the recipient of your messages will see a small signature that says you're on a mobile device. Some phones also support the AIM client for those who want to download and install it on the handheld.

YAHOO! MESSENGER USERS

Setting up your cell phone for instant messages is easy with Yahoo! Messenger. Simply click the Messenger tab at the top of the IM window and select Sign in to Mobile Device. You must first check for compatibility (depending on what country you're in and what service provider you're using) and then register your mobile phone number (see Figure 2.12). Your phone must also be able to accept text messages.

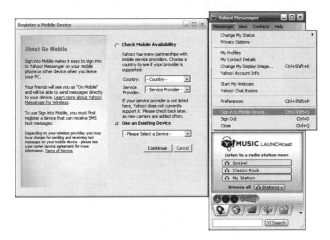

FIGURE 2.12
The shortcut Ctrl+Shift+S will automatically forward your IMs to your mobile phone. The first time you attempt this, however (pictured here), you must select the country and carrier to confirm compatibility, and then register the phone number.

Reproduced with permission of Yahoo! Inc. © 2005 by Yahoo! Inc. YAHOO! and the YAHOO! logo are trademarks of Yahoo! Inc.

If you like, you can choose to automatically sign your mobile phone in when you exit Yahoo! Messenger. To set this up, click Messenger, and then Preferences. Under the General tab, the last option is Always sign into my mobile device when I exit Messenger. Click the box here to activate this option. This feature is grayed out (inaccessible) if you haven't yet registered your mobile phone.

MSN Messenger Users

Open your MSN Messenger window and click the Tools tab at the top, and then select Edit My Mobile Settings. One of your options is Mobile Device. By clicking Mobile Settings, you will be taken to the MSN Mobile website to answer questions such as your service provider, phone number, and so forth. It's a cinch (see Figure 2.14). After this is all set up

Don't Get Caught

There are many ways to slack using your favorite IM program. For example, most offer the capability to play solo or multiplayer games and some let you listen to music channels on your PC. The trick, of course, is not to get caught, so be sure to watch the volume (especially if you're in a cubicle). Figure 2.13 is what the music options look like in MSN Messenger.

(only required the first time), you can choose to have all IMs sent to your phone by clicking Tools, and then Edit My Mobile Settings, and then clicking the box that says Allow people on my contacts list to send messages to my mobile device.

FIGURE 2.13
Most IM programs let users listen to a wide range of commercial-free music. Yahoo! Messenger offers tunes via LAUNCHcast (www.launchcast.com), and pictured here is a glimpse of MSN Messenger's audio selections.

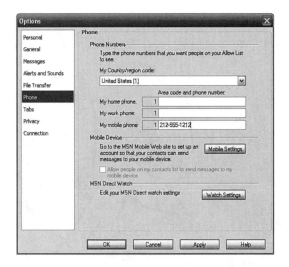

FIGURE 2.14
MSN Messenger users can select if they want messages zapped to their text-enabled cell phone, PDA, or smart watch.

Some IM services will notify you when others are typing something in their IM window. This is a handy feature because you will be informed that a message is coming soon (and thus, you're less likely to type over one another)! With some IM programs, including Yahoo! Messenger and MSN Messenger, this feature is built into the software, whereas with others, such as AIM, users must choose to let others see that you're typing a response (found in the options settings).

Trick the Boss

Okay, this one's a bit of a stretch, but let's say you're supposed to be in one location (for example, your office) but you're really in another (at home). Because all the popular instant messaging programs let you use a webcam for video chats and conferences, if you put some "office stuff" behind your head at home (for example, a cubicle wall, file cabinet, and so on), you might just get away with looking like you're at the office. Just try to prevent your dog from jumping on your lap. Or when you stand up, be sure you're wearing pants!

SLACKING WITH REMOTE ACCESS SOFTWARE...

- Log onto your home PC from work so you can surf when and where you want (without that sneaky IT watchdog on your back).

- Late for work? No one at the office needs to know—log onto your office PC from home and pull up that day's newspaper so it looks like you've already been there!

- Out with your friends at an outdoor patio? No worries—tap away on your PDA and take control over your office PC as if you were right in front of it.

...SO WHAT ARE YOU WAITING FOR, GET SLACKING!

Chapter 3

Remote Access Software, Your Best Friend

• • • • •

Gotta love the Internet. Sure it's a blast to surf the Web, play games against friends around the world, and receive email (with the exception of spam, of course), but the Net can also be used to access a computer from another one elsewhere on the planet. In fact, when you log into your computer remotely, you can control it with a keyboard and mouse as if you were sitting right in front of it! How freaky is that?

And hey, if you have a wireless network at home, you can even log onto your office PC while sunbathing on a lawn chair in the backyard, or while nursing a killer hangover on the couch.

Referred to as "remote PC," "remote access," or "remote control" programs (depending on whom you ask), these tools allow you to remotely connect to another computer to view and edit files, run software applications, read email, surf the Web, and print documents or images at your current location.

ACCESS YOUR HOME OR WORK COMPUTER—ANYTIME, VIRTUALLY ANYWHERE

- Using Symantec's pcAnywhere, you can "see" the contents of your office PC from another Internet-connected computer—even from your comfy chair at home.

- With the web-based GoToMyPC, you can be virtually anywhere and still be "virtually" in the office.

- If you get really desperate, work with what Bill gave ya. Use the Windows XP (Pro) Remote Desktop feature to get to your home computer from work and check those ball scores or do your online shopping where no one can see what you're up to.

Now, this clever networking software is *supposed* to be used for productivity purposes. You know, to do things like access your important work files at the office while you're on the road (using any Internet-connected computer), which eliminates the risk of losing your laptop that might contain valuable information. Or, you can use these programs as a handy way to transfer files from one computer to another. Or say you're having problems with your computer—these programs let a technician "inside" your computer, even if he's in another city (while you watch and learn).

Although there are many programs that let you securely log into one computer using another, three popular products today are Symantec pcAnywhere (www.symantec.com/pcanywhere), Citrix's GoToMyPC (www.gotomypc.com), and Microsoft's own Remote Desktop, a feature built into Windows XP Professional (www.microsoft.com/windowsxp).

Note...

Although the three programs highlighted in this chapter each offer a slightly different way to log onto another PC, and each has its own unique features, all three can be used to perform the most common functions such as view and edit documents, copy files between computers, and access the Web and email.

Now, if we're highlighting these programs in a book on "white collar slackery," you bet we've found ways to use—nay, abuse—this software to get away with some sneaky stuff at the office.

Throughout this chapter, you learn how to do things such as log into your home computer from work so you can surf to all those websites that are blocked at the office (see Figure 3.1).

FIGURE 3.1
If you're unhappy with your job and want to search for a new one, you can scan all the employment sites you like at work—via your home PC—to be extra sure you're not being monitored at the office.

Don't Get Caught

If you want to take the day off—but don't want your customers or clients to know you're at home reclining on your La-Z-Boy—why not use a remote access program to log into your work email address and reply as if you were at the office? It's a sneaky tip for those who can't access their work email from another computer or a mobile device. And no one will be any the wiser.

Here's another idea—how about logging onto your computer at work when you're still at home to pull up that day's newspaper? Therefore it looks like you've already been in the office! Heck, you can even update that website every hour so it seems like your boss or co-worker just missed you! Take a look at Figure 3.2 to see how this looks.

FIGURE 3.2
See the date prominently displayed underneath *The New York Times* logo? A snooping boss or co-worker might stroll by to see where you are. Little do they know you pulled up this website from home when you realized you woke up late. It might just save your butt as you race into work!

And get this—throughout this chapter you'll also learn how to log into your computer from your PDA while you're on the way to the office. No fooling.

Note...

Bored with nothing to do at work except work? If you happen to have music or DVD files stored on your hard drive at home (such as a downloaded flick from a video on demand service like Movielink, CinemaNow, or Real!Starz), remote access software gives you the ability to access those files. Now you can fill that empty afternoon with something other than sales reports and boring meetings. If you're working on a corporate or local area network, a firewall might prevent you from using a remote access program. If this is the case, chat with your network admin about granting access to your home computer (and make a convincing argument why you need it!). If all else fails, buy him lunch. Remember, some employers do not allow any software to be installed on a PC, so unfortunately, you're SOL if this is the case (that is, if the lunch you buy for the IT guy doesn't work).

Considering you're likely using an "always on" Internet connection at home, such as a broadband DSL or cable modem, why not take advantage of this technology to make it look like you're working harder than you really are? This chapter teaches you how to set up this technology for your own purposes (who are we to ask?). To make some sense of this chapter, here's a bit o' terminology: The computer you want to operate remotely is referred to as the "host" computer, whereas the computer that you're using to control the host is known as the "client" computer. Got it? Good.

OK, let's get down to business. The following is a look at what's involved in setting up a remote access connection for each of the three aforementioned programs: Symantec pcAnywhere, GoToMyPC, and Windows Remote Desktop.

Don't Get Caught

Nothing says "slacking" more than wasting a day away by playing a computer game— on someone else's dime. Yes, even if this means the occasional mind-numbing round of Windows Solitaire. Some mean bosses delete all games from office computers, so remote access programs let you log into your home PC from work and play your favorite time-wasters. These apps also let you play web games on the remote computer, should they be blocked on the PC at work.

WORK FROM PCANYWHERE—WITH A LITTLE HELP FROM SYMANTEC

You're probably well aware of Symantec's popular Norton Anti-Virus and WinFax software, but the company also has a leading remote access program, Symantec pcAnywhere.

This $199.95 product can be downloaded from the company's official website (www.symantec.com/pcanywhere) or purchased on disc at retail. It's a one-time fee, opposed to other remote PC solutions such as subscription-based services, such as GoToMyPC (more on this in a mo').

Symantec pcAnywhere provides secure, remote access that supports network connections over a local area network (LAN), wide area network (WAN), or the Internet. It also supports modem-to-modem connections and direct cable connections via a serial or parallel port.

Minimum system requirements for Symantec pcAnywhere include

- CD ROM: CD-ROM or DVD-ROM drive
- CPU Speed: 233MHz
- CPU Type: Intel Pentium
- Disk Space: 32MB
- Display: VGA or Higher
- Memory (RAM): 64MB

Next, you must install the software on both the host and client PC. What, did you forget already? The host PC is the one you want to log into remotely and the client PC is the one you'll be in front of.

Installation, Setup, and Other Stuff You Gotta Do

Assuming you have a constant connection over the Internet, here's how to set it up:

1. Pop in the CD and a splash screen will appear (if your auto-play feature is enabled). Otherwise, go to your CD-ROM drive (for example, D: or E:) in Windows Explorer or My Computer and double-click **setup.exe** to begin the installation. Follow the install wizard. It's all in plain English so it'll be easy to follow (seriously).

2. On the host computer, open the program and from the main menu, click on the word Host by the left side of the screen. Then, right-click over the word Network, Cable, DSL and choose Properties (see Figure 3.3).

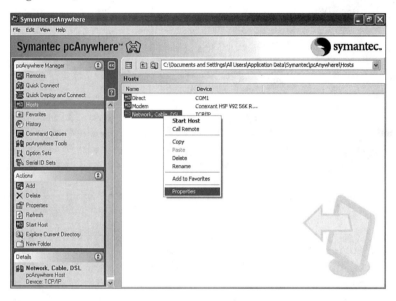

FIGURE 3.3
Easy as pie. This action sets up the computer so that it can be logged into from another computer using the same software. You just need to do this once.

3. Now click the Callers tab and then New Item (the first icon under Caller list) to create a name and password for the connection. Be sure to write this down so you don't forget it (see Figure 3.4).

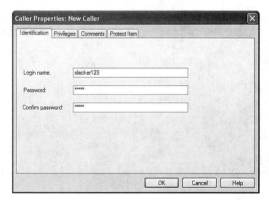

FIGURE 3.4
Here, you set up the name for the connection with the host computer, and a password so that only you can access the computer remotely.

4. Now click OK to get back to the Host screen.

Now if you double-click Network, Cable, DSL, you will see a little blue icon in the lower-right corner of your computer screen (near the clock). If you put your mouse over this little blue monitor with a check mark on the screen, it will say Symantec pcAnywhere waiting. In other words, it is waiting for a client PC to access it remotely.

Note...

Many remote PC products exist in the marketplace—some are available at retail on CD-ROM while others can be downloaded off the Net. They all work relatively the same, however, the current release of pcAnywhere (version 11.5) has ratcheted things up a notch. If you choose pcAnywhere as your remote access option you are getting advanced security features, cross-platform connectivity, better performance and easier connection procedures than some of its counterparts, as well several interface improvements that can definitely make your overall experience with pcAnywhere a positive one.

Before you leave this computer and head on over to the second (client) computer, you need to know this computer's IP address so that the client knows which computer to log into. An IP (Internet Protocol) is the unique numerical identity of a computer or device over a network.

Here's how to find the IP address of the host computer:

1. Be sure you're connected and logged onto the Internet. Then, in Windows XP, click Start, and then Run.

2. Now type **cmd** and then press Enter. At the C: prompt, type **ipconfig** and then press Enter (see Figure 3.5).

FIGURE 3.5
Remember the good ol' DOS days? Even if you don't, finding the IP address of your host computer isn't difficult, and only needs to be done once to allow a client to access this PC remotely.

3. Write the IP address number down or email this silly-looking number to the client computer (where we're off to in a moment).

If you are using a dynamic IP address—therefore the PC's address changes every time you connect to the Net—then you can use a DNS service, such as DynIP (www.dynip.com), which is bundled on the pcAnywhere CD. Otherwise the remote PC won't know which computer to log into if the numerical address is always different.

Note...

If you want to control a computer that exists on the same router as the client (such as in a home network), you do not need to know the IP address of the host computer.

Okay, off to the client computer you go.

1. Install the Symantec pcAnywhere software—just like you did with the host computer.

2. Now open the Symantec pcAnywhere software and click Remotes on the left side of the screen.

3. Then, right-click on Network, Cable, DSL and choose Properties. Choose Settings, and then type the host PC's IP address (see Figure 3.6).

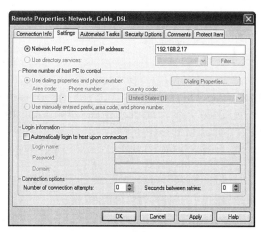

FIGURE 3.6
We know it sounds confusing, so let's cover it again. You need to type the IP address of the host PC on the client computer so that it knows where to log into over the Net.

Note...

If the host computer (say, at the office) is behind a firewall, the remote user must be able to connect to the network through a remote access service (RAS) or virtual private network (VPN). An administrator should be able to provide this information, so don't sweat the details.

You're almost done...really! On the client computer, click Quick Connect on left side of the screen and type the IP address of the host computer. Now what you see is the host computer. Cool, huh? Have fun clicking around and typing to see what you can do.

Now nearly everything that you can do if you were sitting in front of the office PC is at your fingertips—including creating spreadsheets, editing documents, reviewing presentations, and checking email—even though you're on your hammock in the backyard with your wireless notebook!

So much work... so little time

"Leapfrogging" describes using a remote access program, such as Symantec pcAnywhere, to log into one computer (a host) and then using that computer to log into another computer. Now you can transfer files between two other computers altogether. Or, if you don't want your colleagues to know your IP address for security reasons, leapfrogging is a way to keep it a secret (they'll only know the IP address of the second computer in the chain)!

CLICK THAT GREEN BANNER AD! INTRODUCING GoToMyPC

You might have seen this product advertised on the Internet. They're everywhere. Citrix® GoToMyPC® became wildly popular in 2004 for its ease of use, and has since spawned multiple offshoots, such as GoToMyPC Pro and GoToMyPC Corporate. But let's concern ourselves with the consumer model, simply entitled GoToMyPC Personal (www.gotomypc.com).

It should be noted off the top that GoToMyPC works a little differently than Symantec pcAnywhere (see Figure 3.7). Although this software also lets you remotely access your computer, you can do so from any other Internet-connected computer (and many PDAs) in the world, with almost any operating system.

FIGURE 3.7
Here's a visual representation of how GoToMyPC works. Unlike Symantec pcAnywhere, GoToMyPC is a web-based application, therefore any Internet-connected PC can be used to control the host (or multiple hosts if you so choose).

Imagine you're enjoying a latte at you favorite café and it offers wireless access—simply flip open your WiFi-enabled PDA, visit the gotomypc.com Web site, then log into your work computer to edit that presentation you've been putting off. Who says you need to be in your stuffy cubicle at the office? The latest version of Symantec pcAnywhere also lets you control another PC from a Windows Mobile-based PDA.

Let's take a look at what's required to get going:

- First download GoToMyPC to the host computer (the one you want to control remotely). This is a small self-extracting file. The free trial includes unlimited remote access to one computer and expires after 60 minutes of connection time or 30 days, whichever comes first.

- Install the software, which should take about two minutes—tops. Leave your computer on and connected to the Internet.

• Go to another computer and log in to www.gotomypc.com. Enter your email address, password, and access code and then click Connect. Within seconds, your PC desktop will appear in front of you. Now you can begin working on your PC as if you were sitting in front of it—even though you might be halfway around the world. A green window will line the screen to let you know it's the host PC you're seeing. See Figure 3.8 and Figure 3.9 for a sample view.

FIGURE 3.8
After the software is installed on the host computer, visit GoToMyPC.com and type your email address, password (on the left side of the screen), and access code. Within moments, you'll see the host PC as if you were in front of it.

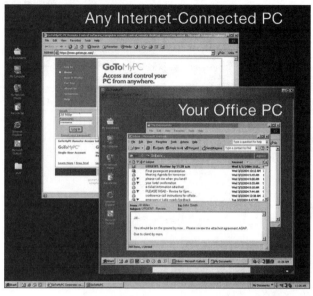

FIGURE 3.9
A green border lining the computer monitor lets users know they're accessing a host PC remotely.

GoToMyPC also differs from Symantec pcAnywhere in its pricing. Although Symantec's product requires a one-time fee, GoToMyPC is a subscription-based service that does not incur any extra connection costs and can be purchased on a monthly or annual basis.

Currently, prices for GoToMyPC Personal are $19.95 a month or $179.40 a year. For two PCs (hosts), it's $29.95 a month or $269.40 a year. Three to 20 PCs are an additional $14.98 per month, for each host PC, or $135.00 a year. If a company wants all their employees to have remote access (more than 20 PCs), they might opt for the aforementioned corporate bundles.

A neat feature with this software is to "invite" co-workers to a remote session—simply by emailing them. In writing this book, a rep from GoToMyPC sent me a message with a link to click. It said: "You have been invited to remotely access Ashley's computer. To access it, you need to down-

So much work... so little time

Why not write it off? Citrix Online says more than 60 percent of their GoToMyPC users are reimbursed by their companies. Now why didn't you think of that?

load the GoToMyPC Viewer. You must be connected to the Internet to join Ashley. To begin, click Start." And that was that. Then, together, we went through various features of this software (see Figure 3.10).

FIGURE 3.10
If you want to invite someone to your PC, simply right-click on the little green & white "MyPC" icon in the corner of your PC screen (near the clock). One option is Invite Guest to PC. Here's a snapshot of what it looks like when you click this selection.

So, how do you use your PDA to access your desktop at work? Simply visit www.gotomypc.com on your handheld device and punch in your email address, password, and access code and you're in. The GoToMyPC software supports these following portable platforms:

- Microsoft Pocket PC 2002

- Microsoft Pocket PC 2002 Phone Edition

- Microsoft Windows Mobile 2002/2003/2003SE

- Microsoft Windows Mobile 2002/2003/2003SE Phone Edition

- Most devices running Microsoft Windows CE 4.0 or later

Don't Get Caught

Because you must collaborate on a business project, your boss says you need to visit a client in another city. But you really don't feel like boarding a plane and traveling 3000 miles when your wife is eight months pregnant (er, and neither does she). What to do? Tell your boss you're on your way. But instead, you stay at home, download GoToMyPC, and invite your client to work together on the same computer. (Or try Citrix Online's new GoToMeeting solution for instant meetings on the fly.) Your boss will be none the wiser (at least, you can hope that's the case). Now you can stay at home for a few days to account for "traveling time." Ahem.

Peering Through the Windows

Windows XP Professional users can take advantage of the integrated remote access software, dubbed Remote Desktop. Just like Symantec pcAnywhere and GoToMyPC, this software lets you control your computer over the Internet while at another computer altogether.

Note...

The Remote Desktop feature from Microsoft is only found within the Windows XP Professional Edition and not the Windows XP Home Edition. That said, both versions support the similar Remote Assistance feature, which allows a system administrator to remotely control your computer for tech support/troubleshooting purposes. If you've ever called the Microsoft technicians for Windows XP help, they might have asked your permission to take control of your computer remotely so that they can show you what they're doing to fix your problem. Also, be aware that any version of Windows (95 or higher) can control another Windows computer via the Remote Desktop feature, but only the computer with Windows XP Professional Edition can be controlled (a.k.a. the "host" PC). Capiche?

The following is a look at what you need to use Remote Desktop:

- Windows XP Professional installed on your host computer—the computer you want to operate remotely.

- A remote (client) computer running Windows 95, Windows 98/98SE, Millennium Edition, Windows NT 4.0, Windows 2000, or any version of Windows XP. This computer must have the Remote Desktop Connection client software installed (more on this in a mo').

- A connection to the Internet, preferably at broadband speeds.

Assuming you've met the requirements, let's take a look at how to set it all up.

Getting Remote Desktop Up and Running So You Can Run Off

First things first—you must enable the Remote Desktop feature on your host computer so that you can log in remotely from another computer (you must be logged on as an administrator or as a member of the administrators group to enable Remote Desktop on your Windows XP Pro-based computer).

1. Click Start, and then choose Control Panel, and then double-click the System icon.

2. Click Remote and then check the box that says Allow users to connect remotely to this computer. Click OK (see Figure 3.11).

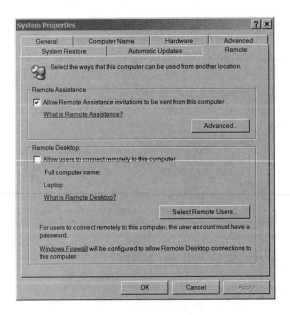

FIGURE 3.11

One quick check and your host computer is ready for remote access.

3. Leave your computer running and be sure you're logged onto the Internet. Now go to another Internet-connected PC.

Now it's time to set up the client so that you can remotely control the host computer. Remember—it works on any version of Windows (95 and newer), but you need the Remote Desktop Connection software.

The client software is selected by default when Windows XP is installed on a PC. In case it was not, it's available on the installation CD for both Windows XP Professional and Windows XP Home Edition.

To install Remote Desktop Connection software on a client computer, pop in the Windows XP Pro CD-ROM. From the welcome page, click Perform Additional Tasks, and then click Setup Remote Desktop Connection, as shown in Figure 3.12. Should you want to install remote desktop software on a client PC without Windows XP, you must download a small piece of software from www.microsoft.com/download. Do a search for "Remote Desktop Connection". This package will install the client portion of Remote Desktop on a computer running any of the following operating systems: Windows 95, Windows 98 and 98 Second Edition, Windows Me, Windows NT 4.0, and Windows 2000.

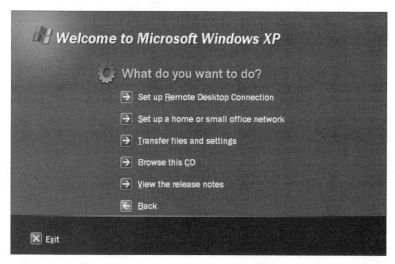

FIGURE 3.12
Don't you wish you kept that Windows XP disc? Simply click Setup Remote Desktop Connection and follow the installation wizard directions.

Let's recap: You've enabled your Windows XP Professional computer to allow for a remote connection. Then, you've installed client software on another Windows-based computer, right? Good. Now you're ready to start a Remote Desktop session.

You must first establish a virtual private network connection or remote access service connection from your client computer to the host computer. Don't worry—it's not that difficult to set this up.

1. On the client computer (the one you are using to access another), open Remote Desktop Connection by doing the following: Click Start, Programs (or All Programs), Accessories, Communications and finally, Remote Desktop Connection.

2. In the blank area by the word Computer, type the computer name if it's on the same network or the IP address of the computer that you want to connect to (be sure that it has Remote Desktop enabled), as shown in Figure 3.13. Then click Connect.

FIGURE 3.13
Tell the client PC which host PC you want to control remotely.

3. The Log On to Windows dialog box appears, so now you must type your username, password, and domain (if required). Click OK.

The Remote Desktop window will open and this computer should look familiar—you're now remotely controlling the host computer. To change your connection settings, click Options before you connect to customize the process.

Note: If your computer is assigned a dynamic IP address, therefore the address of the computer changes every time you connect to the Internet, you should consider a service such as DynIP (www.dynip.com) or Dynamic DNS (www.dyndns.org), so this remote PC program can work for you!

Have fun finding new ways to slack using your remote access program!

SLACKING WITH PORTABLE GADGETS

- Learn how to edit your BlackBerry messages to make it look like you're in your stupid cubicle like you should be!

- Forward your office phone number to a handheld device so that your customers or clients think you're diligently plugging away at the office.

- Copy an entire DVD over to your PDA or cell phone so you can watch *Office Space* while in your office space.

- Or how about faking an incoming phone call so that you can get out of a meeting?

- Learn how to play sound effects on your cell phone so your boss thinks you're stuck on the freeway when you're really just running into the shower!

...SO WHAT ARE YOU WAITING FOR, GET SLACKING!

Chapter 4

Portable Gadgets, Your Office away from the Office

Slacking to Go with BlackBerry, Cell Phones, and PDAs

• • • • •

It's not easy being a white-collar worker today. Not only are you expected to work longer hours (nights, weekends, holidays, you name it), but thanks to mobile inventions such as cell phones, PDAs, BlackBerrys, and GPS devices, your boss can track you down wherever you may be.

Isn't it ironic that "wireless" devices are tethering us to the office even more so than before these inventions debuted? Sheesh.

Yes, portable gadgets might serve as an office away from the office, but they can really impede on your personal life. Don't think this hasn't happened—you could be in the delivery room with your wife awaiting the arrival of your precious bundle of joy, and still be expected to respond to the ringing of the cell phone or buzzing of the BlackBerry (although we all know you're *not* supposed to have these things on in hospitals!).

So, why not turn the tables just a little? For example, these devices can be used to make it look like you're in the office when you're really enjoying a beautiful day on the fairway. And did you know you can copy a DVD to your PDA or SmartPhone? Or, why not join a text-messaging club where members call your boss to get you out of work? Oh yes, 'tis true.

And so this is the topic of discussion in Chapter 4.

FINDING YOUR WAY OUT OF A BLACKBERRY JAM

- Get rid of that pesky BlackBerry signature that tells the whole world you're not in your office replying to email like you said you were.

- Fix the subject line of your emails so that it complies with the look of an email sent from Outlook—just in case you've got a really tech-savvy boss.

- Use my list of BlackBerry shortcuts if by some chance you really do want to get your work done but you want to get it done faster.

Without a doubt, the biggest thing to happen to the white-collar working world is the BlackBerry from Research in Motion (www.rim.com). As opposed to Internet-enabled cell phones where you must log onto a site to "pull" your messages to the phone, the BlackBerry "pushes" email so that the handheld rings or buzzes every time you receive a message. Want to respond? Click Reply using the intuitive thumb-keyboard and then type a note and it's zapped away to the recipient. BlackBerry devices are easy to use and reliable, but they can also be quite addictive little devices (hence the nickname "CrackBerrys").

Because you can set up your office email account to be sent to your BlackBerry, many employees can spend more time out of the office than ever before. But if you believe a tech-savvy co-worker you're communicating with doesn't know you're on a BlackBerry—think again.

How's this, you ask? "But when I send a message, it looks like it's coming from my office email account!" you insist. True, but only to the untrained eye. You see, while someone who receives a message from you might see jdsmith@microsoft.com, there are ways to see whether the sender is *really* in the office.

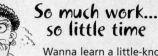

So much work... so little time

Wanna learn a little-known BlackBerry trick? You can choose to receive an email delivery confirmation in both Outlook and on the BlackBerry—so no one slacks on *you*!

Here's how to do it:

From the handheld:

In the subject line of the message, type **<confirm>** followed by the subject. Note: This only works with an email address or the Use Once feature.

From Outlook:

In the subject line of the message, type **<confirm>** followed by the subject.

The following example confirmation message will be received on the handheld and in Outlook:

BlackBerry Delivery Confirmation

Your message,

TO: georgewbush@whitehouse.gov

SENT: Fri Mar 21 10:29:43 2005

SUBJECT: <confirm> we still on for poker?

Has been delivered to the recipient's BlackBerry Wireless Handheld.

Cool!

Why do you want this, you ask? You know, in case someone tries to say they never got your message (we've all used that lame excuse, so why should someone else get away with it!?). This works with any kind of BlackBerry out there.

Goodbye Auto-Signature, Hello Three-Hour Lunch

One way is to take a look at the bottom of the message. By default, BlackBerry messages contain a signature file that says "Sent from my BlackBerry Wireless Handheld." Doh! What—you didn't know that?

Removing the BlackBerry signature at the bottom of every email is a breeze. This isn't performed on the BlackBerry itself, but rather, it's a setting in the BlackBerry desktop software.

Here's how to do it:

1. Open the BlackBerry Desktop Software on your computer. By default, it will be under Start, and then Programs (or All Programs), and then BlackBerry or BlackBerry Desktop Manager.

2. Four icons appear in the window: Application Loader, Back Up and Restore, Intellisync, and Redirector Settings. Double-click on Redirector Settings (underneath the picture of the antennae—see Figure 4.1).

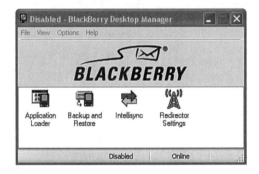

FIGURE 4.1
Although it doesn't sound like the right choice, select the last icon—Redirector Settings—to change (or remove) your auto-signature.

3. Under the General tab (the first tab you should see), the last option will be titled Auto Signature (see Figure 4.2). As you'll see, the default setting is Sent from my BlackBerry Wireless Handheld. Simply delete this entire phrase (and the solid line before it) or choose another signature that doesn't tell recipients that you're not in the office! Cradle the handheld and synchronize.

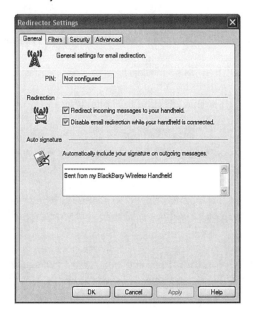

FIGURE 4.2
Simply delete the text in the last window (Auto signature) or replace it with something else.

So, what should you replace your signature with? Hmm, perhaps you want to use one of those fancy motivational quotes that make you sound all brainy and stuff. How about, "Example is not the main thing in influencing others, it is the only thing" (Albert Schweitzer) or "Everyone is trying to accomplish something big, not realizing that life is made up of little things" (Frank A. Clark). Either way, there's no chance anyone will know where you really are when you reply to messages.

Note...

Now, do you love your BlackBerry? Of course you do. But you could be more productive with it. For example, wouldn't you like to get more done in a shorter amount of time? Then you can do more of what you really want—sleeping, for instance (this is where all new parents hypnotically nod in agreement).

So, take note of the following shortcuts—they apply to the BlackBerry 6200 series, the BlackBerry 6510, the BlackBerry 6700 series, and the BlackBerry 7200 series:

- Press C to create a new item when in Messages, Calendar, or Tasks.

- Hold Alt and roll the trackwheel to scroll horizontally in any function to type or view text.

- When typing text, hold a letter key and roll the trackwheel to scroll through the accents, symbols, or marks associated with that character. When the desired character appears, release the letter key.

- When typing text, press the Symbol key to scroll through the accents, symbols, or marks associated with that character. When the desired character appears, click the trackwheel to select it.

- To cut and paste text, press the Alt key and click the trackwheel, and then roll the track-wheel to select text. Click the trackwheel again and select Cut or Copy from the menu. To paste the selected text, place the cursor in an editable field and click the trackwheel. Now click Paste.

- Click the Escape button to exit any menu, dialog box, or screen.

- Press the first letter of an item in an options list or menu to move directly to that item.

- To find a contact when in the To field of a message or in the Find screen, type the first few letters of a name, or type the contact's initials separated by a space.

- Hold a letter to capitalize. The Key Rate option must be enabled from Options, Screen/Keyboard.

- Press the Space key or Symbol key twice to insert a period when typing text (the letter following the period is capitalized automatically).

- Press the Space key or Symbol key to insert the @ and period characters in an email field.

- Press R in an open message or in the Messages application to reply with text to the sender.

- Press F in an open message or in the Messages application to forward a message.

- Press L in an open message or in the Messages application to reply to all recipients.

- Press the Symbol key to open the Select Symbol screen. Press the associated letter below the symbol to insert it.

- Press the Enter key to move down a page in an open message. Press the Alt key and the Enter key to move up a page.

- Press the Alt key and the Right Shift key to turn on CAPS-lock mode. Press the Shift key or Alt key again to turn it off.

- Press the Alt key and the Left Shift key to turn on NUM-lock mode. Press the Shift key or Alt key again to turn it off.

- Press the Alt key and the O key to view outgoing messages. Press the Alt key and the I key to view incoming messages.

- To select Yes, No, or Cancel from a pop-up dialog box, press Y, N, or C, respectively.

- Press the Alt key and the Hotkey in the Messages or Saved Messages screens to carry out a search that you have defined.

- Press the Space key or Symbol key on the Select Folder screen, when a folder marked with a plus sign is selected, to expand and collapse the subfolders.

- Press the Enter key on the Select Folder screen to file a message in the selected folder.

HIDE BEHIND THE SUBJECT

If you want people to think you're using Outlook at your desk (when you're really nursing a hangover in a hotel room), be aware some technically savvy folks will see you're on a BlackBerry—if you don't watch your step.

When you receive an email message in Outlook and respond to it, the subject line (for example, "report") now has a "RE:" in front of it "RE: report". But did you know that when you reply to a message using a Blackberry, it adds a "Re:" in front of the subject like "Re: report", instead? Don't see the difference, you say? The Outlook response has an "RE:" all in capital letters, while on the BlackBerry only the "R" is capped. If the recipient (such as your boss) is knowledgeable enough, he or she will catch on to your little scheme. So be sure to change "Re:" to "RE:" in the email's subject line, before you send that reply!

Be sure not to tell too many people about this trick, as it's a little-known gem!

Trick the Boss

Oooh—this is a good one. You know all the BlackBerry advice thus far has been how to make it look like you're in the office when you're really somewhere else? Well, if you think about it, you can also fake out someone if you want them to think you're away from the office when you're really sitting at your desk! Scenario: You're supposed to be working on a project but you're so swamped that you haven't begun it yet. If your boss didn't see you come into the office, why not email him or her from your desk and write "Still caught in that nasty pile-up off route 401—will get to that project ASAP!" Now, the trick is to manually write an auto-signature at the bottom of the message: "Sent from my BlackBerry Wireless Handheld." Aha! Clever, eh? And don't forget—if you're replying to a message, be sure to manually change the "RE:" in the Outlook subject field to "Re:" as that's how it'll appear on the BlackBerry!

Get Sports Updates Right on Your BlackBerry

If your boss sees you scrolling through your BlackBerry messages while in your cubicle, he might think you're actually checking work-related messages. Little does she or he know that you're actually reading about your favorite sports, thanks to a product called BerrySchedules (www.BerrySchedules.com). For example, the Pro Football Schedule is a mobile schedule for the BlackBerry that features the complete NFL season schedule by week, by team, and full-season. What's more, all schedules automatically adjust to your time zone. BerrySchedules also offers scheds for college football and pro hockey and basketball. The product is free to try; $9.95 to buy (see Figure 4.5).

```
WEEK 1        All Times Are EST
THURSDAY, SEPTEMBER 10, 2004
Indianapolis at New England, 9:00 pm

SUNDAY, SEPTEMBER 13, 2004
Arizona at St. Louis, 1:00 pm
Baltimore at Cleveland, 1:00 pm
Cincinnati at N.Y. Jets, 1:00 pm
Detroit at Chicago, 1:00 pm
Jacksonville at Buffalo, 1:00 pm
Oakland at Pittsburgh, 1:00 pm
```

FIGURE 4.5
Are you ready for some football? This product from BerrySchedules.com is a handy app that displays the complete NFL season schedule so you'll never miss a game. Work, shmirk!

Put the Mobile Back into Your Mobile Phone

- Instantly teleport yourself to another location by using fake "noises" in the background of your cell phone calls. Choose from options such as car noise, "outdoor" sounds, a phone ringing, and much more!

- Using Verizon's new iobi Home product, you can be on the go and still get calls, email, text messages, and more—without having an "all-in-one" device.

- Is all that slacking giving you some spare time to fill? Try out some of the most popular games that can be played on a cell phone.

There are three things we don't leave the house without: keys, wallet, and our beloved mobile phone. Problem is, not only do we rely on our cell phones, but so do our bosses! Just because technology lets us be reached wherever we are on this planet doesn't mean we should be. But it's too late to go back to the pre-'90s days of stationary communication.

So, why not have a little fun with your cell phone, then?

SOUND EFFECTS—YOUR INSTANT ALIBI

Here's a scenario: You're supposed to start work at 9 a.m. sharp but after a night of heavy partying, you forgot to set your alarm so you wake up at 8:52 a.m. (with your tongue stuck to the top of your mouth). What to do? Call your supervisor or boss on the cell phone and explain that you're stuck behind a huge collision and you'll get there as soon as humanly possible. Now, imagine your story could be supported with traffic jam sound effects that matched your excuse? A clever European application called SounderCover—or Soundster in the U.S. (www.soundster.com)—plays

Trick the Boss

Whether you're trying to get out of work, a family obligation, or a dreaded date with someone who isn't taking the hint, a new text-messaging club might be for you. More than 3,500 folks have formed an "Alibi and Excuse Club" in which one member lies on behalf of another. Now you can text someone when you're in bind and tell 'em to call your boss. They can say something like your aunt Mildred passed on in Phoenix and you need to attend the funeral. Hey, what are friends for (see Figure 4.6)? If you want to inquire about joining, simply visit www.sms.ac/clubs, select United States—Adult, and then type "alibi" in the search window. Joining is free. Later on in this chapter you'll read about a similar—yet more automated—approach, designed for the Treo handsets.

FIGURE 4.6
How will the boss ever know that voice on the phone really wasn't your doctor?

sound effects in your phone so that you sound like you're in one place when you're really in another (see Figure 4.7)!

FIGURE 4.7
Ah, it's good to be a slacker in the 21st century. Products such as the SounderCover let you choose a background noise to fake your location. Clever, huh?

This clever program lets you easily drop in a background sound effect during any incoming or outgoing call so that it gives the impression you're actually in the environment where the background sound is normally heard! (see Figure 4.8).

Don't Get Caught

If you're out and about and want to make it sound like you're really in the office, be sure to use a headset as it'll cancel a lot of the background noise. If someone says, "Are you on your cell phone?" just laugh and say, "No, I'm using one of these hands-free headsets at my desk." If they insist you could say your handset is broken.

FIGURE 4.8
Per the icon at the top of the cell phone screen, SounderCover is active, so simply press the down button during a call to initiate the selected sound effect.

You can pretend you're at the doctor's office, caught in a thunderstorm, in the park, or even at a circus parade! A favorite is the "phone ring" sound—the person on the other end of the line will hear a phone ring so that you can tell them you need to go ASAP because you're expecting an important call. Hmm, this is perfect for when customers are asking where their delivery is and you forgot to send it out!

You can even use your own prerecorded sounds, or sound files downloaded from the Internet.

What's more, Soundster allows you to assign fake environmental sounds to anyone in your address book. You can also simply pick a sound when they call, or when you call them.

The selected Soundster noise is launched once you press the Down key/arrow on the phone whenever you call someone (or when you receive a call). A notification will appear on top of your phone's screen to confirm that Soundster is active.

If you want to try before you buy, there's a downloadable demo—but they don't loop, so they're only played once during the call. The full version retails for $4.99 for the application (with three or four sounds) and $2.99 for additional sounds.

Be sure to visit www.soundster.com to see the long list of supported devices.

Set Yourself Free with Verizon's iobi Home

If you crave the freedom to, ahem, "work" anywhere you like then there's a silly little four-letter word you might want to be acquainted with: iobi (pronounced "eye-oh-bee").

iobi Home from Verizon is an inexpensive monthly service that consolidates your landline, cell phone, and email—and helps people find you instead having to juggle multiple lines of communication from different sources.

iobi Home lets you email voice-mail messages, schedule call forwarding to any phone, or tell your PC to hold your calls. You're thinking, "So, how can this help me slack?" Imagine you've got a date with your golf clubs but you're supposed to be working in your four-foot-square cubicle you call an office. With iobi Home, you can forward your work telephone number to your cell phone so you can close that deal while putting on the green (don't think it hasn't been done!).

iobi Home lets you

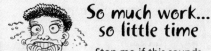

So much work... so little time

Stop me if this sounds familiar—you're trying to get together with someone at work because you're supposed to cooperate on a project—but the guy is avoiding your calls because he didn't do what he was supposed to. Of course, the phones in your office all have Caller ID so you can see who is calling, so that's why that jerk in sales isn't picking up the line. Here's the solution—call your boss's extension and when you speak to his/her assistant, play dumb and say, "Oh, sorry, I was trying to reach Phil in sales." Then ask if you can be forwarded. Now, when Phil sees the boss's name on his call display, you bet he'll pick up the extension! Sneaky, eh? Try it!

- Listen to voicemail right on your computer desktop or email a voicemail clip.

- Send a text message—without a cell phone. Simply log into your iobi Home account and type the message using the intuitive interface.

- Take advantage of the call display features so you can see who's phoning and choose to answer, ignore, or block the call.

- Tag incoming phone numbers and add them to your address book.

- Call forward to any phone. Or how about the ability to schedule call forwarding on your calendar! You know, just in case you've got a hot lunch date a week Thursday!

- Access all this information from any Internet-connected PC or telephone in the world.

To find out more about iobi Home, including an animated demo and a quick test to see whether the service is available in your area, visit www.verizon.com/iobi.

This landline service costs $7.95 a month and can be used to forward to any cell phone—not just ones tied to Verizon Wireless.

PAY IT FORWARD

Most cell phone carriers let you call-forward your mobile phone number to another phone altogether, such as a landline. Some companies charge a flat rate per month for this feature, while others charge for each time you forward. Why do you want this, you ask? What if you're planning to spend Friday afternoon at your buddy's house playing Texas Hold 'Em poker, but when you get there, your cell battery's low? Quick, forward your cell number to his landline so your boss, client, or customers can reach you. As far as they know, you're still working. Just remember to unforward the number when you leave or you'll be busted!

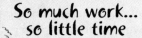

So much work... so little time

Although you might not be aware of it, chances are your cell phone has a three-way calling feature, which can come in handy. Why not impress the boss with it? If you're on your mobile phone and the boss wants to know if that sales projection is ready, call that slacker in your office to put him on the spot. Better yet—don't tell him the boss is on the phone and see what he says about him or her! Okay, this should work with most phones—call the first party, and then enter the second number on the keypad. Press Send, and the first call will wait on hold while the second number connects. After the connection with the third party is made, press Send again to bring all three of you on the line together.

Do you live in the Great White North? Canadian subscribers to Bell Canada or Bell Mobility (www.bell.ca) can easily call-forward their phones—landline or cell phone—to another number by punching in a few simple keys. For the first time, simply press *72 and then enter the 10-digit number you want to forward your phone to. If it's a cell phone, press Talk, and you will hear a long tone—this means the forwarding function has been successfully activated. So now you can spend the afternoon at that special someone's house you met the other week—but have all your office calls forwarded there (your customers won't know the difference)! To unforward, press *73. You will hear the same long tone again, indicating the forwarding function is now off. What's neat is that the phone will remember the number, so if you use the forwarding function again, you simply need to press *72—and not enter the 10-digit number. But, should you want to reset the forwarding number, go back to the first step. Here's two other neat facts about this feature. With Call Forwarding on, you can still use your phone for outgoing calls. And, incoming calls are forwarded to the number you choose even if your phone line is busy.

FUN WITH CELL PHONE GAMES

Did you know your cell phone is all you need to play the latest digital diversions?

Okay, so its small screen and lame sound might turn you off, but cell phone games sure come in handy when you need to waste a few minutes (especially on company time). The following are a few recommended solo and multiplayer games.

To find out which phones are supported, how to download them to your phone, and for how much (it varies between carriers), visit the game's corresponding website.

- **NFL 2005 (Jamdat; www.Jamdat.com)**—Handheld sports games have come a long way since Coleco Head-to-Head Football. Jamdat's pro pigskin sim features all 32 NFL teams and rosters, and includes a deep playbook with dozens of offensive and defensive maneuvers to chose from. Jukes, tackles, fumbles, and snaps—it's all here.

- **Might & Magic (Gameloft; www.gameloft.com)**—Fans of fantasy role-playing games will find refuge in this magical single-player adventure that's spread over 15 huge and colorful 3D levels. Set out on an epic journey to battle foes, solve puzzles, and unravel the mystery that haunts the world of Erathia. D&D nerds, eat your heart out.

Don't Get Caught

Did you know you can even watch live TV on your cell phone? The first company to offer this liberating service is MobiTV (www.mobitv.com). Imagine having access to 22 stations such as Fox Sports, NBC, ABC News, and TLC (so you can watch *While You Were Out*, er, while you were out). They even have a 24-hour stand-up comedy channel! Up to 10 frames per second means the video isn't shabby, and the TV playback on newer handsets is getting faster and smoother all the time. Works with about 20 phones on Cingular and Sprint networks; the cost is a flat $10 per month. Visit MobiTV.com for more information.

- **Joust (THQ Wireless; www.thqwireless.com)**—Save your quarters—this "old skool" classic looks, sounds, and plays just like the arcade version, but now it's small enough to fit in your pocket. Fly your ostrich around increasingly tough levels, while pouncing on winged enemies and running over eggs before they hatch. Also includes cooperative play for two gamers and an Internet high-score list.

- **Phil Helmuth's Texas Hold 'em (Summus; www.summus.com)**—Anyone who's studied the World Poker Championships on television and thought "this guy's an idiot" can now see how'd they fare with this mobile version of the popular poker game. After you can beat the tough A.I. opponents, it's time to log online and test your skill on multiplayer tables (dark sunglasses and cheesy moustache not necessary).

PDA AND SMARTPHONE TIPS

- Get out of a meeting or other such uncomfortable situations with FakeCall 1.1.

- Use LightWav on your PDA to provide "atmosphere" noise in the background while you're on the phone with your boss or a nosy cube-dweller.

- Watch your favorite DVD on your PDA instead of watching all those PowerPoint slides go by when you have to be stuck in that boring meeting.

- Switch over to playing games on your PDA if you've worn out your cell phone battery.

Mobile professionals often rely on a personal digital assistant, or PDA, or one of those fan-danged SmartPhones. As the name suggests, a SmartPhone is a, well, smart phone—a device that offers more functionality than a regular ol' cell phone.

Naturally, there are ways to slack off using PDAs and SmartPhones—everything from listening to MP3s with an earpiece (who would suspect it as it's not an iPod?), to playing games and a handful of applications that can be used and abused in order to slack off.

Let's start with a really sneaky product: Fake Call.

WANNA GET OUT OF A MEETING?

We've all been there—sitting in a boardroom at a long, drawn-out meeting. It's so boring that you'd rather stick pins in your eyes, and—to make matters worse—it's one of those "mandatory" meetings that doesn't involve you in any which way.

How convenient would it be if you received an "emergency" phone call just as the meeting was about to go into its third agonizing hour. If you own a Treo handset, or any other palmOne-based smart phone or Internet-enabled PDA, you can pull this off with a little help from FakeCall 1.1 (www.toysoft.ca/fakecall.html).

This application from Toysoft, Inc. gives you the excuse you need to duck out of a meeting prematurely. Simply hold down a predetermined key on your handset and within seconds that "call" will come to your rescue!

Better yet—FakeCall lets you even preset a time when the call will come.

The call can even play one of four different "hellos" when you answer, so someone sitting beside you won't suspect a damn thing. You can also set it up to play virtually any audio ringtone, be it a MIDI, wav, mp3, ogg, or wma file.

See Figure 4.9 for a peek at what FakeCall looks like.

FIGURE 4.9

Owners of palmOne-based SmartPhones, such as the popular Treo, can fake an emergency phone call during a business meeting (or an awkward blind date) by setting these easy-to-follow parameters. The last image on the right is what it looks like when the phone is ringing.

Requirements include a PalmOS 5.0 operating system and higher and about 250KB of free memory.

FakeCall is free to download and try for 14 days, after that it costs $10.95. But then again, money is no object when you've got slacking to do, right?

GET YOUR PDA IN ON THE SLACKING

Speaking of Toysoft, Inc., the Calgary-based company has another clever slacking tool that is similar to the SounderCover app mentioned earlier in the chapter—but this one is for PDAs.

Owners of palmOne-based personal digital assistants can play sound effects while on the phone to trick the person on the other end into thinking they're in one place when they are not.

LightWav (version 3; $16.95) lets users play a sound effect while on the phone. So if you want to tell your boss you can't make it in because your baby is quite ill, be sure to have that crying baby noise in the background (that sound is sure to get anyone off the phone in a jiffy). Oh, to make sure this works, remember you really do need to have a baby at home or your boss might be just a tad suspicious.

Another great sound effect is plain ol' static. "Sorry, boss, I can't hear you—I'm entering that tunnel near the freeway! Gotta go. See you soon!" Ahem. Time to get your butt in the shower.

LightWav, which is free to try, allows you to associate any uncompressed wave file, mp3, ogg, or wma file to any application (see Figure 4.10). Simply press the corresponding button and the person on the receiving end will be none the wiser.

  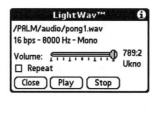

FIGURE 4.10

Toysoft's LightWav can play sound effects such as a traffic jam, annoying static, or a baby crying—whatever you need to get out of a sticky situation! Simply associate the sound file to a given application.

In order to get the sound effects onto your PDA's external card (such as a SD card), you'll need to find sound effects online (make sure they're not copy protected) or you can create your own sound effects with your PDA's microphone or a digital recorder.

LightWav requirements are as follows:

- PalmOS 5.0 and higher with Sound Manager
- SonyClie PalmOS 5.2.1 with Sound Manager
- 190KB of free memory
- External card such as SD/MMC, Compact Flash, or Memory Stick
- Uncompressed wave files

An optional program is PocketTunes 2.1 or higher to play mp3, wma, and ogg files.

This product is compatible with the Palm Tungsten T/T2/T3/E/C and Palm Zire 31/71/72; Treo 600 series; Sony Clie with Palm o/s 5.2.1 and higher; Garmin or Tapwave Zodiac.

Read more about the product at www.toysoft.ca/lightwav.html.

Note...

There's an easier solution for travelers who find they're spending too much time searching for wireless networks in cafés, airport lounges, and hotels. Kensington's Wi-Fi Finder Plus ($29.99) is a keychain-sized doo-hickey that sniffs out wireless networks with the push of a button. If it's green you're good to go; if it's red, no such luck. The market's only Wi-Fi detector means you no longer need to boot up your PC to detect a 802.11b or 802.11g signal (see Figure 4.11).

FIGURE 4.11
About the size of a credit card (just thicker), the Kensington Wi-Fi Finder Plus can detect available wireless networks up to 200 feet away. Read more about this clever product at www.kensington.com.

DVDs in the Palm of Your Hand?

How cool would it be to be sitting in on a meeting, and while all the other white-collar zombies are staring at the stupid spreadsheet projected on the wall, you've got *Spider-Man 2* playing on your PDA?

Believe it or not, a Dutch software company, Makayama Software (www.makayama.com), has a number of products that let you watch DVD movies on your Pocket PC/Windows Mobile-based personal digital assistant (see Figure 4.12). In fact, the software lets you rip a DVD movie on your computer and shrink it down small enough to fit that full-length feature film on a 128MB memory card!

While similar products have existed in the past, DVD to Pocket PC does not require any special software to be installed on the PDA itself, plus the end result is a high-quality video experience that is viewed sideways on the PDA for that "widescreen" landscape mode.

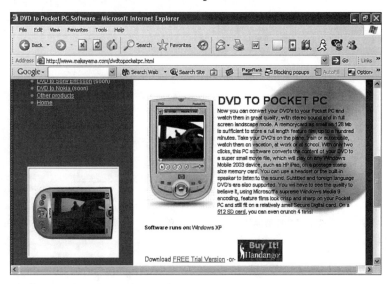

FIGURE 4.12
Talk about a fun way to slack—you can watch your favorite movies on your PDA with this funky tool from Makayama Software. You can lug around four full-length films on a single 512MB memory card. Now that is bloody cool.

All you need is

- A PC with Windows XP and built-in DVD-player.

- One gigabyte of free hard drive space to store a temporary file.

- Pocket PC with Windows Mobile 2003.

- A memory card (Compact Flash, SD or MMC, and so on) with at least 128MB of space. (If the movie runs longer than 100 minutes, or for better picture quality, a 256MB card is required.)

DVD to Pocket PC is free to try, but $27.95 to buy.

A version for the Palm was in the works at the time of writing this book, so be sure to check www.makayama.com to see if it's available.

Here's a quick guide on how to do it:

1. Pop a DVD in your Windows XP-based PC, click Open, and select the Title (the one with the longest duration), as shown in Figure 4.13.

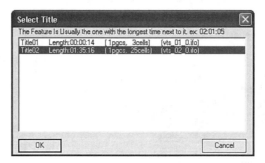

FIGURE 4.13
The first step in copying the movie to the hard drive is choosing the Title with the longest duration.

2. You'll now see the DVD start playing in the Preview window. Choose between normal quality (128MB card) or high quality (256MB or higher).

3. Click Action and the PC will start copying the movie. This is performed in two stages. First, the video and audio from the DVD will be "ripped" or extracted to a temp file on your hard drive.

Note...

This process can take several hours, so perhaps you want to do it before you crash at night. Secondly, this huge file (about 1 gigabyte) will then be compressed down in size before dragging and dropping the file onto your PDA's memory card. This should start automatically. If it doesn't, you might need to reboot your PC, then launch the DVD to Pocket PC software and select Special, and then Step 2 Run from the Options to start the process manually.

4. When the conversion is finished, you'll see a file called DVD.wmv on your desktop. Simply rename it to the movie (for example, Shrek 2.wmv) and now you're ready to copy it over to your PDA's memory card. If the PDA is connected to the PC in its cradle, you can cut and paste it into the memory card directory on your Pocket PC; a 100-minute movie should copy over in about two minutes. You might also use Active Sync, and click Explore and Copy to Storage Card.

5. On your PDA, open Windows Media Player and click Playlist. You will see your file (for example, Shrek 2.wmv) and you can tap it to play.

Play around with the various settings to tweak the audio and video (see Figure 4.14).

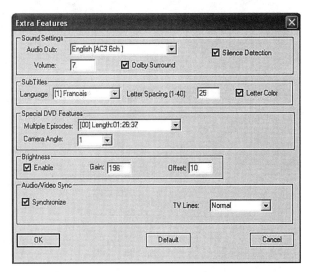

FIGURE 4.14
Once the movie is on you can adjust various settings such as audio options, subtitles, and zoom modes.

That's it! Neat, huh?

Note...

As anatomically impossible as it is to have brains on your wrist, that's essentially what the MSN Smart Watches are. Keep track of weather, news, sports scores, stock quotes, and Outlook calendar appointments—all on your wrist. The MSN Smart Watch technology is built into a few new high-tech timepieces from the likes of Fossil, Tissot, and Suunto ($150 to $700 for the watch; $9.95/month for service) that can receive up-to-the-minute information—wirelessly—in more than 100 U.S. cities (and 12 Canadian cities). And get this—if your boss is looking for you, your friendly co-worker on MSN Messenger can zap you a note to get your butt back to the office ASAP! Dick Tracy, eat your heart out. See Figure 4.15 for a couple of options. Visit www.msndirect.com for more information.

FIGURE 4.15
Interestingly, the wireless info delivered to the watch is via a slice of an available FM radio signal. Watches are the first devices supported by Microsoft's "SPOT": Smart Personal Objects Technology.

PDA Games Galore!

What chapter on mobile slacking would be complete without a look at some of the hottest games for your palmOne- or Pocket PC-based PDA?

Owners of PDAs need not lug around a Game Boy as there are thousands of downloadable diversions available for your pocket computer instead. The following are just a small handful of recommended picks, each tested rigorously for a high "fun factor." Hey, it's a tough job, but someone's gotta do it. Happy tapping!

Candy Cruncher

Playing with food has never been this much fun. In Candy Cruncher, gamers must line up similar sweets to create columns or rows. This is achieved by dragging adjacent candy types using the stylus pen. After a complete row of jellies, jawbreakers, or candy watermelon slices are aligned, they disappear; a predetermined number of rows or columns must be completed before the clock runs out. In total, there are 15 candy types, with new ones revealed every few levels or so. The dreaded black hole means that space cannot be swapped with other candies, and will prevent a row or column from being completed. Candy Cruncher is extremely addictive—without the calories.

(Astraware; for palmOne- and Pocket PC-based PDAs; free to try, $14.95 to buy; www.astraware.com.)

AntHill

Many gamers might recall dumping quarter after quarter in the '80s arcade game, Ms. Pac-Man. Well, the world's first digital heroine (sorry, Lara Croft) is back again—in spirit anyway—with this clever clone, dubbed AntHill. You know the rules: munch as many dots (er, ant eggs) on the board as possible while avoiding the subterranean creepy crawlies. But eating one of the four power pellets reverses the chase. Then players have a limited amount of time to snack on the monsters. This remake features colorful graphics, multiple levels of game play, fun sound effects, a High Score board, and the ability to control the game either by the Pocket PC's buttons or a stylus pen.

(BallShooter Games; for Pocket PC; free to try, $9.95 to buy; www.ballshooter.com.)

Dope Wars

While selling drugs might get you 5 to 10, if you're plugging away at the ol' 9-to-5 and need a coffee break, pull out this fun, adult business simulation. The goal of the controversial Dope Wars is to buy and sell a number of narcotics while avoiding cops, thieves, rival gangs, and so forth. Players start off with a limited amount of cash and a sizeable debt before tackling one of six locations to push their wares. The game isn't much to look at—it's primarily text-based—but mature gamers looking for a challenging biz sim will have fun tapping away at this digital (and legal!) addiction. And hey, because the game is grayscale and only 14KB, it's perfect for older Palm PDAs.

(Matthew Lee, for palmOne PDAs; free; www.download.com.)

Scrabble®

Word game fanatics, rejoice! The world's most popular word game can now be played in the palm of your hand for one to four opponents (see Figure 4.16). That is, gamers can play solo against the computer or challenge up to three human opponents. Features include the ability to save a game in progress, a "friendly" mode (whereby the computer can suggest a next move), support for two Palms to play wirelessly, and a built-in 100,000+ word *Official Scrabble Player's Dictionary*.

(For palmOne- and Pocket PC-based PDAs; free to try, $19.99 to buy; www.handmark.com.)

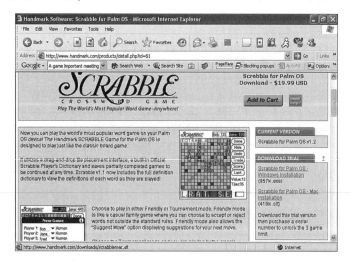

FIGURE 4.16

The classic Scrabble board game has gone mobile—this PDA version can be played against the smart computer AI or against a friend on the same PDA or another one, wirelessly. Can you spell C – O – O – L ?

Hyperspace Delivery Boy!

In this adventure game, players become Guy Carrington, fresh on the job as a courier for the Hyperspace Delivery Service. It's your job to deliver important parcels throughout the known universe—even if it means crossing paths with deadly robots and devious aliens. The full version of the game includes 30 levels, a choice between puzzle or action modes, plenty of secrets to uncover, and impressive graphics.

(For Pocket PC-based PDAs; free to try, $19.99 to buy; www.monkeystone.com.)

Bejeweled/Diamond Mine

Bejeweled for the palmOne or Diamond Mine for the Pocket PC is the same game—and proves to be one of those rare puzzle diversions that's easy to pick up but impossible to put down. Simply use the stylus pen to drag and drop adjacent jewels so that three or more of the same form a vertical or horizontal line (see Figure 4.17). When this happens, they disappear, causing more colored crystals to drop onto the screen. Top scorers can post their best performance on the Internet for all the world to see—and beat.

(For palmOne- and Pocket PC-based PDAs; free to try, $14.95 to buy; www.astraware.com.)

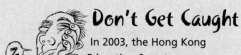

Don't Get Caught

In 2003, the Hong Kong Education Secretary was allegedly caught playing Bejeweled on his PDA during a lengthy legislative meeting. The poor shmoe was caught by student representatives who were seated one row behind the education chief. Apparently, Professor Li was unapologetic for playing the puzzle game on his PDA.

FIGURE 4.17
Tap n' go! Bejeweled is as much fun on a portable digital assistant as it is on your PC. Drag and drop same-colored jewels so that three or more are aligned vertically or horizontally.

Text Twist

Easily one of the most addictive word games is Astraware's Text Twist for color or grayscale PDAs. In this timed game, six scrambled letters appear on the screen and it's the player's job to see how many three-, four-, five-, or six-letter words they can make within two-and-a-half minutes. If a six-letter word is made, the player automatically advances to the next level. In total, there are 10,000 words in the game's database so don't expect to see the same words over and over.

(For palmOne- and Pocket PC-based PDAs; free to try, $14.95 to buy; www.astraware.com.)

Note...

Don't forget—in Chapter 3, "Seeing Is Believing," I discuss how to use those clever "remote access" programs to control your work PC from a PDA or SmartPhone! Imagine accessing all your files or pulling up spreadsheets when you're sipping a cold beer on a patio instead of slaving away at the office.

SLACKING AND COVERING YOUR TRACKS...

- Don't you love all those online games that can help you slack the day away? Learn how you can hit the "panic button" when the boss walks by so that you can continue your game, or other slacking activity, when he or she is around the corner.

- Worried that the boss might be snooping around in your browser history to check up on you? You can get rid of any trace of where you've been online, what files you had open, and more.

- Want to avoid any other possible clues to your daily slacking activity? I'll show you how to duck and cover by hiding your taskbar, using fake screensavers, playing work "noise" through your PC's speakers, and running fake installation programs that all make you seem like you're the office "go getter."

- Find out how to encrypt select files and folders so that your boss or co-workers can't access them.

...SO WHAT ARE YOU WAITING FOR, GET SLACKING!

Chapter 5
More Slacking Bites and Bytes
Other PC Tips and Tricks

● ● ● ● ●

So far we've covered how to use email, IM programs, and remote access tools to make it look
like you're hard at work when you're really just, well,
slacking off.

Guess what—this is just the beginning.

Throughout this chapter you'll find countless other
ways to use your PC to help pass the time at the
office. You know, for those days when the clock's
hands actually seem like they're moving *backward*.

I'll show you how to cover your web surfing tracks so
your boss can't see where you've been surfing to on
company time. You don't need to be a computer
engineer to learn how to erase web history and other
revealing information on your office PC.

Or, how about changing that game of Solitaire into
an image of a spreadsheet with the click of one button? Yep.

You'll even find out how to create a screensaver that looks like you're working when you're really at the local mall shopping for an anniversary gift. Over the following pages, you'll also learn about programs that create audio sound effects (such as typing) through your computer speakers when you're really catching a catnap!

Other fun things in this chapter include a list of the top free downloadable computer games for when you're itching for a new digital diversion—and some handy tips on how to find what you're looking for online so that you can get your work out of the way to play these recommended games.

Finally, we'll chat with "the Don" of slacking—Don Pavlish—whose website, Don's Boss! Page (www.donsbosspage.com), has helped untold employees get away with slacking.

Okay, let's start off with the ol' "panic button."

Trick the Boss

There's an age-old keyboard shortcut you should know if you don't already. It's called the "Alt+Tab shuffle." Use your left thumb to hold down the Alt button (just to the left of the spacebar), and then use your left forefinger to tap the Tab button. By doing so you can quickly toggle to another opened program on your computer so it hides what you were just doing. For example, you might be playing a heated game of Tetris or perhaps looking for a new job at a website. If the boss or a nosy co-worker walks by, you can quickly pull up a PowerPoint presentation that was open in the background! And if your boss has a discerning eye, later on in this chapter you'll see how to hide your taskbar at the bottom of the screen so that your boss doesn't see what programs are open.

PANIC BUTTONS ARE FOR YOUR SECURITY—JOB SECURITY, THAT IS

- Take advantage of free "Personal Protection" at Don's Boss! Page.

- Find games, such as the popular time-waster Snood, that have panic buttons built right into the program!

- Use more sophisticated software, such as History Kill, which features a handy panic button among other handy tools.

All you want to do in life is play Euchre. Is that too much to ask? Well, it seems like little things such as a roof over your head, food on the table, and clothes on your kid's back are considered "important" these days. Sigh. Well, maybe there's a way you can do both.

Dozens of websites offer free multiplayer games of Euchre and it just so happens that you work in front of a PC all day long. How convenient. The trick to doing both, however, might be to download a "panic button" so the boss doesn't catch on to your dirty little secret. He or she walks by, so you click a button to pull up a spreadsheet that shows a sales forecast. It's a win-win situation. Ahem.

GET PERSONAL PROTECTION AT DON'S BOSS! PAGE

You can find—and download—panic buttons at various websites that support the slacking cause. For example, Don's Boss! Page (www.donsbosspage.com) has one called the Personal Protector that acts as a companion when you're surfing the Web. As the site says, the Personal Protector "makes the web safe for countless man-hours of lost productivity"!

Simply head on over to www.donsbosspage.com/protector.shtml and then click the button that says Launch My Protector. A small rectangular window will stay on your screen (you can drag it anywhere you like). This floating window offers various jokes and factoids about slacking, while the bottom of this window has a prominently displayed Boss button in green (see Figure 5.1).

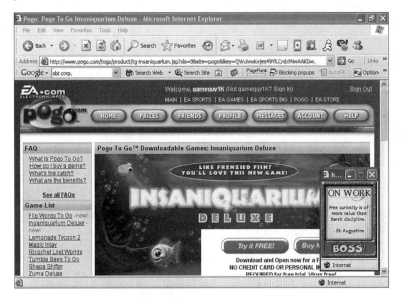

FIGURE 5.1
Surf the Web to your heart's content knowing you can protect your job with the click of a button.

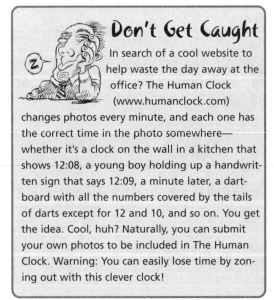

Don't Get Caught

In search of a cool website to help waste the day away at the office? The Human Clock (www.humanclock.com) changes photos every minute, and each one has the correct time in the photo somewhere— whether it's a clock on the wall in a kitchen that shows 12:08, a young boy holding up a handwritten sign that says 12:09, a minute later, a dartboard with all the numbers covered by the tails of darts except for 12 and 10, and so on. You get the idea. Cool, huh? Naturally, you can submit your own photos to be included in The Human Clock. Warning: You can easily lose time by zoning out with this clever clock!

Boss coming? Click the panic button now. As the boss takes a peek over your shoulder, you're seemingly working on the company's revenue projections—just like he asked you to do this morning (see Figure 5.2). Just make sure he doesn't get to examine this screen too closely!

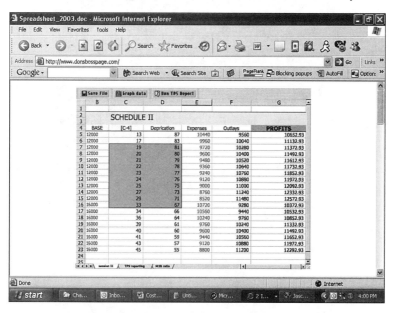

FIGURE 5.2
Because the panic button stays on top of your browser at all times, it'll always be in reach when the boss strolls by. Clicking it launches a fake spreadsheet such as the one seen here.

PLAY GAMES WORRY-FREE WITH BUILT-IN PANIC BUTTONS

Some popular computer games, such as Snood (www.snood.com), have built-in panic buttons. As you see in Figures 5.3 and 5.4, if you simply press the Y key during the game, it will pull up a spreadsheet! Perhaps Y stands for "Yikes!" or "Y can't you let me finish this level?"

When the coast is clear and you want to start playing again, press the Y key a second time. If you need to exit the game, click the X in the top-right corner of the game to close it.

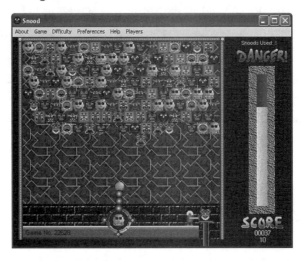

FIGURE 5.3
Snood is a very popular time waster. One of the new features added in version 3.5 for Windows is a handy panic button for when the boss strolls by.

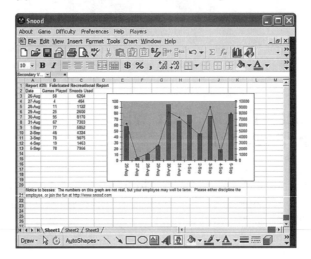

FIGURE 5.4
Sneaky, huh? Simply press the Y key during a game of Snood for Windows and this is what you'll see.

KEEP YOUR ONLINE ACTIVITY OUT OF SIGHT

Some panic buttons work in different ways. A program called HistoryKill 2003 (www.historykill.com), for example, hides all browser and IM windows—even minimized ones—so that passersby can't see where you've surfed to or what you're up to. HistoryKill is free to try for 15 days, and then users are asked to cough up $39.95 to keep using the software.

Here's how its panic button works. First, download this free program at www.historykill.info/boss-key.htm. It's about 2.3MB in size.

After you double-click to install it (see Figure 5.5), you can choose what you'd like to hide when you click the panic button.

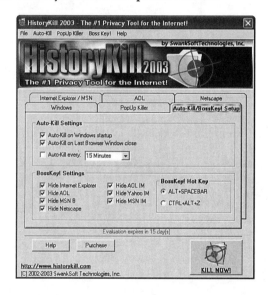

FIGURE 5.5
On the Auto-Kill/BossKey! Setup tab, check the boxes for the windows you'd like to close if someone comes by your desk. You can also select from one of two panic button hotkeys.

Dirty jokes, dating websites, and venting forums for disgruntled workers are probably not the kind of websites the boss wants you to visit on company time (see Figure 5.6). Now, say you're surfing to a few sites you shouldn't be visiting. If the boss strolls by, simply tap Alt+Spacebar or Ctrl+Alt+Z and all will be hidden (see Figure 5.7). Want to go back to secret surfing? Just press the panic button again.

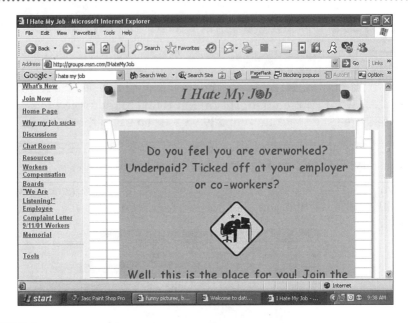

FIGURE 5.6
If someone approaches, tap the magic panic button and all web browser windows will disappear.

FIGURE 5.7
Nothing to see here, folks! Just a harmless desktop wallpaper of your baby boy. Better yet, make sure you have a work-related program open, such as a Word or Excel file.

Similar products include the free The Panic Button (www.a2zhelp.com) and the more robust Anti Boss Key, (www.mindgems.com), which is free to try; $14.95 or $29.95 to buy (depending on the version).

Panic buttons also exist for webmasters, too. Don's Boss! Page also offers one of these (see Figure 5.8). The site asks "Say someone's looking at your site from their workplace when the big cheese walks by. You wouldn't want that person fired for surfing the net on the job, would you?"

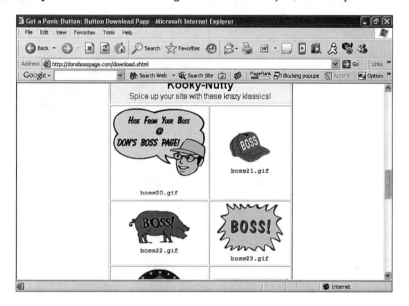

FIGURE 5.8
From the main menu at Don's Boss! Page (www.donsbosspage.com), click Wire Your Website, and then download a panic button of your choice. Examples of some of the different ones are shown here.

Adding one of these panic buttons to your website is a simple process. After you choose and download a desired button (.gif image), upload it to your server and then add the provided HTML code to your web page (see Figure 5.9). Then, email Don to tell him about it and he'll add your site to his list of recommended links!

Trick the Boss

If you don't want to download an office "panic button" program, at least hide your current web activity the old-fashioned way—open your browser and call up your company's website. Now minimize it so you see the tab at the bottom of your screen on the taskbar. Now go to another website—the one you really want to visit during office hours—but if someone comes, quickly click the button to maximize your company website (or press Alt+Tab) so it covers any other windows you have open.

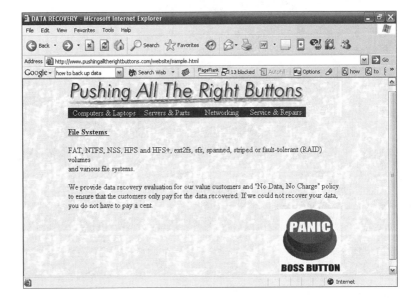

FIGURE 5.9
Pictured here is an example of a web site with one of Don's custom panic buttons. If needed, Don also provides the line of code required to add it to your site.

ERASE YOUR HISTORY, COVER YOUR TRACKS

- Cover your tracks the quick and easy way by using a software program dedicated to the preservation of your slacking ways.

- Can't install software on your work PC without authorization? The manual alternative to the process is not as foolproof as the software-assisted clean up, but still worth a shot to cover your tracks.

- Got a snoopy boss or coworker? Protect your personal files and folders from those prying eyes by encrypting those "important" files.

Even though you might be swift enough to close the browser window when your boss passes by your cubicle, you may be leaving traces of your whereabouts on your PC. And hey, your boss (or the IT department) might decide to check up on what you've been up to.

Thankfully, there are dozens of programs on the Internet designed to erase your Internet history with just one click. They can delete your URL history, cookies and temporary cache files, and more.

After all, finding out where you've been online is very easy for your boss or IT guy to do—unless you do something about it. Don't believe me? Open your Internet Explorer browser (the world's most popular browser at more than 90 percent market share) and press Ctrl+H. Or click View at the top of the screen, and then choose the Explorer tab, and then History. As you'll see in Figure 5.10, all your surfing activities come up on the left side of the screen. Busted!

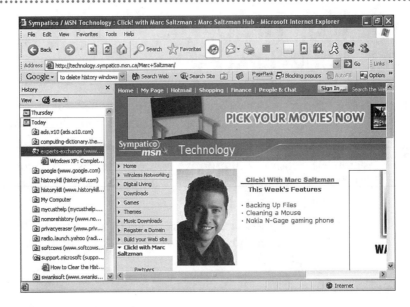

FIGURE 5.10
As the Guns n' Roses song says "It's so easy!"—to find where you've been online, that is. By pressing Ctrl+H in your browser, your snooping boss will see where you've been.

TERMINATE YOUR HISTORY AND AVOID A TOTAL RECALL

Free programs to handle this mess include Don't Panic! (www.panicware.com), History Swatter (www.historyswatter.com), History Eraser (www.123Stay.com), and Evidence Wiper (www.operationsystems.com).

A more comprehensive program is HistoryKill 2003, the software mentioned earlier in this chapter for its "panic button" feature. But this clever suite of tools does a lot more, especially for those who want to cover their tracks (see Figure 5.11).

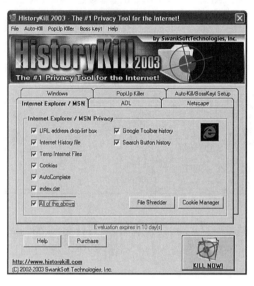

FIGURE 5.11
HistoryKill 2003 is very easy to use—simply click off what you want to be erased from your PC by checking off the desired box(es).

And its file shredder feature encrypts and overwrites your web surfing tracks at least 21 times so that no one can undelete or recover your web tracks (see Figure 5.12)! According to the company, HistoryKill defeats forensic software used by the U.S. Secret Service, the U.S. Customs Department, and the Los Angeles Police Department!

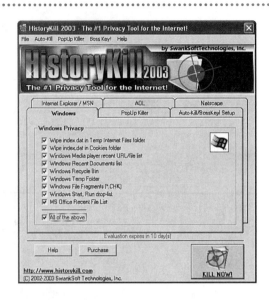

FIGURE 5.12
Even more options for those savvy enough to know what they do. Bottom line? You might not want your boss, co-workers, or your IT snob to know where you've been while using the office computer.

In Figure 5.12, you might have noticed cookies as an item HistoryKill 2003 can wipe. Just in case you aren't familiar with that term when it comes to web browsing, let's give it a quick run down. Cookies are small files written to your browser by certain websites. Typically, they're used to identify or authenticate a user of a website without requiring them to sign in again every time they access that site (so they're not always such a bad thing). But if your boss visits a site from your computer and it greets you by name, he or she will know you've been on there before! With HistoryKill, you can choose which cookies to get rid of and which ones are okay to keep—that way you don't end up having to log into sites that would be deemed acceptable at your work place (see Figure 5.13).

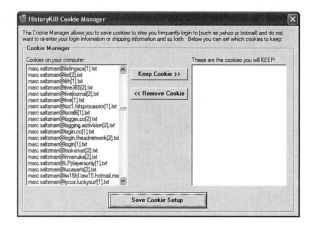

FIGURE 5.13
Take a look at the kind of trail you leave when surfing the Net. Cookies will show all!

HistoryKill 2003 also removes the following:

- AutoComplete history

- Browser history

- Browser cookies

- Temporary Internet files

- Address drop-list box data

- Recycle Bin files (does this automatically at Windows start up)

- Windows Media Player recent files and URLs

- Temp folder files

- Windows fragmented files

Don't Get Caught

If you're the type to count down the hours, minutes, and seconds to 5 o'clock, why not make it a little more exciting by downloading and installing a countdown timer? It'll feel like New Year's everyday (party hats and champagne are optional). Both of these websites offer countdown clocks: www.thecountdownclock.com and www.contactplus.com (look under "Free Stuff"). And hey, why not use them for weekends or holidays, too? It's celebration time.

- Windows recent documented list (automatically at Windows start up)
- Windows Start, Run menu lists (at Windows start up)
- MS Office recent file lists
- index.dat files (a HistoryKill exclusive)

If you don't remove these, Windows automatically accumulates them and remembers every Web site you visit and every file you open.

Other good programs used to automate the process of covering your tracks include

- No More History (www.nomorehistory.com)
- Window Washer (www.webroot.com)
- Privacy Eraser Pro (www.privacyeraser.com)

You can likely find free trials of these kinds of programs at www.download.com.

Don't Despair, Try Manual History Removal

If you'd rather delete history yourself instead of using one of these dedicated programs, there's good news and bad news. The good news is that it's not too difficult to do, but the bad news is that you can't wipe away anywhere near what you can with the history removal programs, such as HistoryKill.

Let's look at a couple of examples.

To clear the History folder (in Internet Explorer 4.0 and newer), do the following:

1. Click Internet Options on the View (or Tools) menu at the top of the web browser screen to open the Internet Options dialog box.
2. Click the General tab, and then click Clear History.
3. Click Yes, and then click OK (see Figure 5.14).

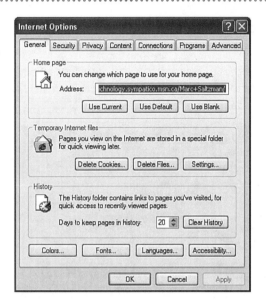

FIGURE 5.14
After cleaning up your history, you can also delete cookies and temporary Internet files here. See—that wasn't so hard, was it?

Many folks who use the popular Windows Media player (www. windowsmedia.com) for music and videos know that when you launch the program, it will automatically cue the last thing you listened to or viewed (simply press Play and you'll see for yourself). Well, if you don't want someone to know what you just saw or heard—and have access to other history information embedded in this program's memory—it's time to remove it (see Figure 5.15). To wipe clean the recent media files launched by Windows Media Player 9 and up, follow these steps:

1. Open Windows Media Player and click Options under the Tools menu.

2. Click the Privacy tab.

3. Click the Clear History button to clear Windows Media Player's recently played files list.

4. Click the Clear CD/DVD button or Clear Caches button to clear Windows Media Player's recently played CDs, DVDs, and media stored on connected portable devices.

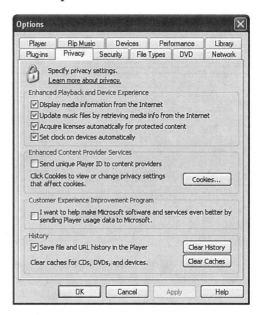

FIGURE 5.15
Click the Clear History button and no one who uses your computer after you will know what video clips you watched at work.

Note...

In case you glossed over Chapter 3, "Seeing Is Believing" remember that "remote access" programs (also referred to as "remote PC" or "remote control" programs) are also ideal for covering your tracks while surfing the Internet. Because you're logging into another computer (for example, at home) to surf the Web from your office, there isn't a way to track where you've been after you log off the remote PC application!

PROTECT YOUR PERSONAL FILES AND FOLDERS

We all know we're not *supposed* to use our office PC for personal reasons, but hey, we're only human after all. And considering we're devoting much of our waking life to the company (and making someone else rich!), we in fact earn the right to use our PC for private reasons—whether it's playing games, listening to MP3s, editing photos of the kids or, er, writing a résumé.

And hey, protecting files and folders isn't such a bad idea for sensitive work files, either—especially on a laptop in case the PC is stolen or lost.

The following step-by-step instructions are for Windows XP users. And as you'll see, it's a lot easier to set this up than you might think.

Here we go:

1. Open Windows Explorer. You can do this by either right-clicking on the Start button and selecting Explore, or clicking Start, and then selecting All Programs, Accessories, Windows Explorer.

2. Once inside Windows Explorer, right-click a file or a folder that you want to encrypt. Now, click Properties.

Note...

Remember, you can select multiple files in Windows by holding down the Ctrl button while you click all the files you want to encrypt. Then right-click the group of selected files to make the change to all the files/folders at once rather than one at a time.

3. Click the General tab. Look to the bottom-right and you'll see a button that says Advanced. Click it. One of the options near the bottom is to encrypt contents to secure data. Click to check this box.

Note...

Files or folders that are compressed (such as MarcsStuff.zip) cannot be encrypted, nor can files with the System attribute or any files in the system root directory structure. This is for your protection, anyway, as it could screw up your PC's performance.

4. If you choose to encrypt a file, you will be asked if you want to encrypt the entire folder that contains it as well. Similarly, when you encrypt a folder, you'll be asked if you want all files and subfolders within the folder to be encrypted, too.

Now, when someone else logs onto this PC they will not be granted access to the selected file(s) or folder(s)! If they try to open a document, for example, it will say "Word cannot open the document: Username does not have access privileges (drive:\filename.doc)." If someone tries to copy or move the document from the encrypted folder to a portable media (CD-R, USB flash drive, and so on) or elsewhere on the PC, a message will appear that says "Error Copying File or Folder."

If you're experiencing difficulty encrypting files or folders, visit support.microsoft.com for technical help. Or you can click Start, and then select Help and Support.

If you want to password-protect your files rather than denying access based on the Windows username, you can do so by compressing files and selecting to add a password to view the contents of the zipped file. Learn more about this by clicking Start, and then selecting Help and Support. Alternatively, you can read instructions online at support.microsoft.com. Type **compress files** into the search window.

OTHER FUN TIPS FOR SUCCESSFUL SLACKING

- Even if you've successfully followed all the other advice in this chapter, that pesky taskbar could blow your cover. Find out how to get that thing out of sight.

- Thought screensavers were a thing of the past? Think again. Find out how to use a screensaver to not only save your monitor but also save your job!

- Learn about programs that fool your boss or co-workers into thinking you're installing a program on your computer whenever you're not around!

When there's a will, there's a way.

This portion of the chapter addresses ways to edit your Windows settings to better hide your slacking, plus you'll read about clever programs that take slacking to the next level.

HIDE YOUR TASKBAR FROM PRYING EYES

Those little minimized programs, files, and website addresses displayed at the bottom of your screen are tell-all signs about what you've been doing while on your office PC. This area is referred to as the Windows *taskbar*.

Sure, the contents of these minimized windows might not be that noticeable to a casual passerby, but it's nobody's business what you're doing on your PC (okay, so it *might* matter to your boss). Let's take a look at what you can do to eliminate this little problem.

You can easily change the taskbar settings in Windows so that it is always hidden—until you run your mouse over the area. This is known as the "auto-hide" feature.

To turn it on, right-click anywhere on the taskbar but make sure it's on the taskbar itself and not on a minimized web browser window or minimized file (for example, digital photo) or program (for example, calculator). The best area to do this is near the Start button on the left side or near the clock on the right side. After you right-click on the taskbar, you will see the last option is Properties. Click on it.

When the Taskbar and Start Menu Properties dialog opens, click Auto-hide the taskbar (see Figure 5.16) and click OK. After a moment, you'll see the taskbar vanish from the bottom of the screen. Simply move your mouse down to the very bottom of your screen and it will pop up again. Voila! Now if your boss asks you why your taskbar is hidden (if she or he even notices), just play dumb and say something like "Oh, yeah, I noticed something was weird. How do I change it back?"

FIGURE 5.16
Auto-hiding the taskbar hides the programs, files, or websites you have active or minimized at that time. Click the box to auto-hide the taskbar so you can't see it until you move the mouse down to it.

Once inside the Properties area shown in Figure 5.16, you might also choose to unlock the taskbar, which means you can make it thicker by clicking on its top edge, holding down the mouse button then dragging it up. Or you can choose to put it on the top or sides of your screen instead of on the bottom. Another option here is to clump all related programs together so having multiple browser windows open at the same time ("multitasking web surfing") means all the URLs are together in one group at the bottom of the screen rather than separately and side by side. Gotta love options.

Do you have your taskbar on the side or top of your computer screen instead of along the bottom? No worries—the aforementioned advice works regardless of where the taskbar is.

FUN WITH SCREENSAVERS

 Did you know you can use screensavers to slack off? How's this, you ask? First, the basics.

Unless you've been living under a dusty Commodore 64 for the past 20 years, you know that a screensaver is designed to lengthen your PC monitor's lifespan. By displaying moving pictures or words on a computer's monitor, screensavers prevent a stationary image from burning into the screen's picture tube. These programs usually start after the computer has been left idle for a few minutes and will stop once the keyboard or mouse is touched.

While most operating systems ship with a bunch of screensavers already installed—and there are thousands to download off the Net—you don't really need them any more thanks to advancements in monitor technology. Nevertheless, they're a personal statement as you can choose something that represents, well, you. Do you have fish swimming peacefully across the screen or characters from the video game *Halo 2* blasting each other into next week? You get the idea.

Okay, now imagine you stepped out of the office to, I dunno, visit your sick mother in the hospital (or so you tell the co-worker you're trying to impress). Problem is, when you leave your PC, your screensaver will kick in after a few minutes so anyone who walks by your cubicle will know you haven't been around. You don't want the boss to notice, do you?

So, here's an idea: What if you could create a screensaver that displays spreadsheets or other company-related files or images so that it doesn't look like it's a screensaver. Now, that's an idea! And guess what—it's easy as pie to set up.

Here's what you need to do.

The first step is to pick one document, spreadsheet, or anything that you'd like displayed on your screen when you're not around.

Better yet—choose more than one spreadsheet and have the screensaver cycle through it every few minutes so it looks like you've returned to your desk and now you're working on something else!

After you've selected your document/file of choice, you need a way to turn it into an image file, such as a .jpg. .bmp., .tif, and so forth. The easiest way to do this is to download one of the hundreds of "screen capture" programs available on the Internet. All these let you press a predetermined series of keys (called a hotkey) to take a snapshot of what's on your computer screen. It then saves it as an image file to your hard drive.

Screen capturing programs include the popular HyperSnap DX (www.hyperionics.com), Screen Capture (www.screen-capture.net), or the free Screen Hunter Free (www.wisdom-soft.com). You can find a whole bunch of these programs by going to www.download.com and typing "capture" or "screen capture" in the search window. Some imaging programs such as JASC's Paint Shop Pro (www.jasc.com) also have a built-in screen capturing function.

After you've taken a snapshot of a Word file or spreadsheet, drag and drop it/them into your My Pictures folder using Windows Explorer (see Figure 5.17). It is found inside your My Documents subfolder, usually found in the Documents and Settings folder.

FIGURE 5.17
Copy or move the image of your spreadsheet program or any other work-related file into your My Pictures folder. This is the first step to creating this sneaky screensaver!

After this is completed, go to your desktop (the screen you see when Windows first boots up) and anywhere on the background/wallpaper, right-click and select Properties. This brings up the Display Properties dialog box. Now, select the third tab, Screen Saver.

Click the option labeled My Pictures Slideshow (see Figure 5.18) and you'll see your image displayed in the little window here. If there is more than one selected, you will start seeing them rotate. Here, you can choose how long each photo should stay on the screen before going to the next one.

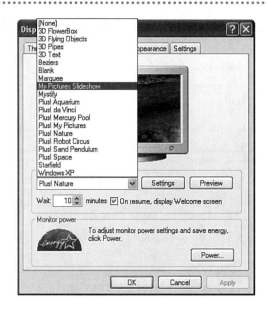

FIGURE 5.18
The My Pictures Slideshow is a screensaver that's built into Windows XP, so try it out before paying to download other slideshow-based screensavers available on the Net.

But wait—I'm not done yet. You need to tweak the settings to get going. Click the Settings tab (see Figure 5.19). Drag the first slider all the way to the right so that your images change every three minutes (the maximum time allowed in this free screensaver). If you only have one image saved to the My Pictures folder, ignore that slider. Now drag the second slider all the way over to the right so that your image will be displayed at full screen (as if you were really using it).

Now, uncheck both Show File Names and Use Transition Effects Between Pictures as these options might ruin the realistic effect. Leave all the other settings alone. Click OK, and then click Apply and you're good to go!

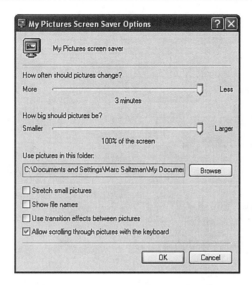

FIGURE 5.19
These are the Settings of the Windows XP My Pictures Slideshow screensaver.

Note...

If you prefer to keep these images in another folder other than My Pictures you can do so, but you need to tell your screensaver to look in another folder for the images. You do this by clicking the Browse button on the My Pictures Screen Saver Options dialog box (seen previously in Figure 5.19) to browse your hard drive for the desired folder.

If you can't be bothered to password-protect your PC or power it down when you step away from your desk, here's a fun way to send your snooping boss or co-workers a message. The free Don't Touch My Computer Episode 2 (http://enetwork.ncbuy.com/downloads/ntcdtmc2.html) is a cute animated screensaver that shows a cute little lovable dog who occupies his time by chasing his tail or scratching himself silly. However, if someone sits down at your computer and touches your mouse or keyboard—watch out. This dog pounces at your monitor and barks loudly! For full effect, crank your PC's speakers before you leave your desk (see Figures 5.20 and 5.21). Did I mention it's free?

FIGURE 5.20
In the free Don't Touch My Computer Episode 2 screensaver, Joe drops off his seemingly friendly dog who just wants to hang around. Right? Wrong.

FIGURE 5.21
If anyone touches your mouse or keyboard—this cute pup turns into a fierce guard dog! Yikes!

PC Audio Tricks

At Don's Boss! Page (www.donsbosspage.com), the savvy webmaster provides a number of audio sound effects to fool your co-workers or boss into thinking you're hard at work (when you might be catching a catnap).

From the main web page, click Sound Busy (or go there directly at www.donsbosspage.com/sounds.shtml) and take a look at these four clever audio clips:

- "Plain Ol' Typing" sounds like you're typing away furiously on your PC's keyboard. Your co-workers will nod in amazement. They'll say "That guy Mike is always hard at work!"

- "Phones from Hell" makes it sound like your desk/office/cubicle is bombarded with phone calls (so no one will bother you).

- "Typing and Whipping" makes it sound like a slave driver is standing over your desk while you're trying to do your work (sound familiar?).

- "Just Whipping Please" offers a straightforward whipping sound effect if you're trying to make a point about your boss.

You can play each of these clips in mono or stereo sound and they should work right inside your browser window when you click it (see Figure 5.22). Simply select one of the eight options (two per sound effect) then click the little arrow button to play the clip. Great stuff.

FIGURE 5.22
What a terrific idea—at Don's Boss! Page (www.donsbosspage.com), you can play sound effects, such as typing or phones ringing, so passersby think you're a tireless worker. Thanks, Don!

FAKE INSTALLATION PROGRAMS CAN CREATE USEFUL BREAK TIME

What—you thought this chapter was finished already? Sheesh. I'm just getting warmed up!

A clever but little-known program called Nap 'n Coffee (http://kinkodev.free.fr) makes it look like you're installing a program on your computer whenever you're not around. It's a free tool created by Azrael for The Kinko Development Zone in France.

Here's how it works—when you first double-click the file to install the program to your hard drive, it asks you to name a shortcut that will appear on your desktop. For example, you might call it "Defrag" or "Back-Up Files" or "Current Projects" or something similar that sounds official.

When you've named this shortcut, head back out to your desktop and you'll see the icon waiting for you. Double-click it and the Nap 'n Coffee Control panel screen will pop up (see Figure 5.23).

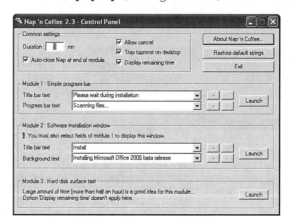

FIGURE 5.23
With Nap 'n Coffee, a free download from the Internet, users can create fake installation screens on their computers for when they're away from the helm.

You can select how long this "installation" should take (default is five minutes). Then, you can choose from one of three customizable "installation" views. The first two are similar (one is a small window and the other is full screen), but they both ask you to choose what it should say on your computer while it's doing it. This includes text such as "please wait during installation," "setup," "copying files", or "defragmenting files" (see Figure 5.24).

FIGURE 5.24
Doesn't this look authentic? Another option is a full screen size installation dialog box. How sneaky. I love it.

A third option is for when you're going to be away from your computer for a long while as it shows a fake "disk defrag" screen called a "Disk Doctor—Surface Scan" module (see Figure 5.25).

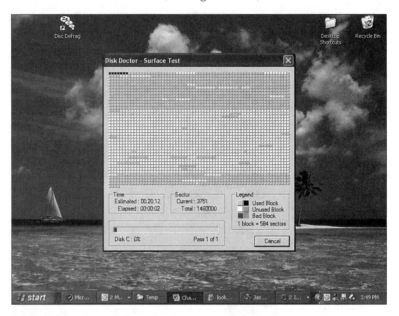

FIGURE 5.25
If you know you're going to take a while having a smoke outside, this is the best one to use. After all, everyone knows you shouldn't touch your computer when you're defragging the hard drive, right?!

Note...

A web version with a similar phony installation screen exists, but it isn't as customizable as Nap 'n Coffee, plus you need a browser window open to see it (see Figure 5.26). Still, it's worth checking out—even with its silly headline that's a dead giveaway it won't work! You can find the website here: http://www.jasperfforde.com/games/bosscoming.html.

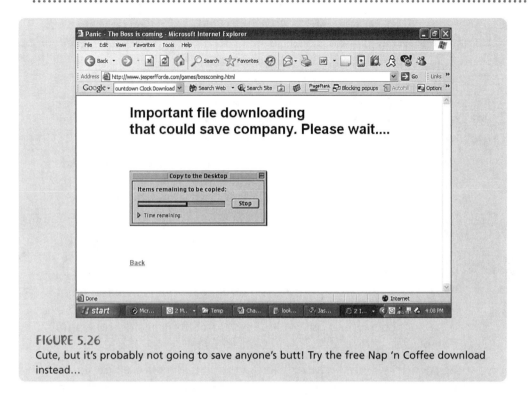

FIGURE 5.26
Cute, but it's probably not going to save anyone's butt! Try the free Nap 'n Coffee download instead...

TEN TIPS TO BETTER WEB SEARCHING

"And I Still Haven't Found What I'm Looking For"—U2, 1987

If the title of this popular '80s ditty summarizes your experiences on the World Wide Web, you're certainly not alone.

Like a needle in a haystack, it can be very difficult to find anything specific on the Internet among its billions of web pages.

You might be asking yourself—why is this in a book about slacking? Well as you're probably aware, the faster you can get your work done, the more time there will be to slack off (and you'll be less likely to get caught).

So consider these following ten tips to help you find what you're looking for in cyberspace. Take heed to these little-known searching tips, tricks, tweaks, and techniques (not listed in any order):

- Almost all search engines, including Google, have an "advanced search" area that provide web surfers with more options. Here, users can search by date or look for websites with a specific domain (for example, .net, .edu, or .tv) or find websites in a preferred language.

- To better help the search engine find what you're after, you can search for a sequence of words that must be in that order. You do so by placing the phrase in quotation marks. For instance, those looking for information on the TV show *Saturday Night Live* should type "Saturday Night Live" into the query window. Without quotations on each end, a search engine will likely search for websites containing any of the words: Saturday, night, and live.

- Be specific! If broad words yield too many results (for example, car classifieds), try more specific words to find what you want such as used car classifieds, Mercedes classifieds, or Miami car classifieds.

- If your keyword(s) do not yield the results you're after, try synonyms. A free thesaurus is available at Roget's Thesaurus (www.thesaurus.com) or Merriam-Webster OnLine (www.m-w.com). After all, a dog is also a canine, a pooch, a mutt, a hound, a pet, and man's best friend!

- This following trick should work in most search engines. Put a plus sign ("+") in front of a word that must be found in the search. Here is an example: city guides +Chicago. Similarly, you can put a minus sign ("–") in front of a word that should not appear in the results, such as python –Monty, if you're only interested in snakes or the programming language and not the British comedy troupe.

- If you know the website you want to search but aren't sure where the information is located within that site, you can tell Google to only search that domain. Do this by entering what you're looking for followed by the word "site" and a colon followed by the domain name. For example, to find admission information for the University of California, Los Angeles, enter this: admission site: www.ucla.edu.

- If you're after quality and not quantity, there are a few search engines that provide access to hand-picked "Best of the Net" sites. One example is About.com at, you guessed it, www.about.com.

- If you prefer not to have adult sites included in your search results, activate Google SafeSearch inside Google's advanced search page. While not 100 percent accurate, sites that contain explicit sexual content are eliminated from the search results.

- If you do a lot of searching during your web surfing, consider downloading free toolbars that always sit near the top of your browser window. This way, you do not need to leave the website you're on in order to type in a new query. Very handy! For example, there's the Google Toolbar (toolbar.google.com), Yahoo! Toolbar (toolbar.yahoo.com), and MSN Toolbar (toolbar.msn.com).

- Lastly, keep in mind there are many specialized search engines, as well. Google, for example, has Google Images (images.google.com) for searching for pictures, Froogle (www.froogle.com) for shopping-related websites, and Google News (news.google.com) for thousands of published news articles from around the world. You can find many more "specialty" search engines at searchenginewatch.com.

FREE GAMES TO SLACK OFF WITH

The Internet houses some fantastic PC games that are free to download and play—perfect for those who need to slack off during the ol' 9-to-5 grind.

Sure, there are thousands of web games in cyberspace, but these recommended downloads offer deeper game-play, plus they let you play offline and you can copy them to your laptop for your next business trip, too (virtual golf at 30,000 feet, anyone?).

Called *freeware*, these games are full, unrestricted versions, so there are no limitations on game play and length or those nagging registration screens that you get in try-before-you-buy "shareware" titles.

The following sections offer a peek at a few recommended freebies to help pass the time. Other recommended freeware games include Bethesda Softworks's The Elder Scrolls: Arena (www.elderscrolls.com), Steel Panthers: World at War (www.steelpanthersworldatwar.com), and the classic adult time-waster, Dope Wars (www.beermatsoftware.com).

MORAFF'S MOREJONGG 3D

Based on the ancient Chinese tile game *Shanghai*, Moraff's MoreJongg 3D (www.moraff.com) is an addictive puzzler that challenges players to correctly match and remove two similar tiles from a pile, but only the ones on the top and sides are accessible (see Figure 5.27).

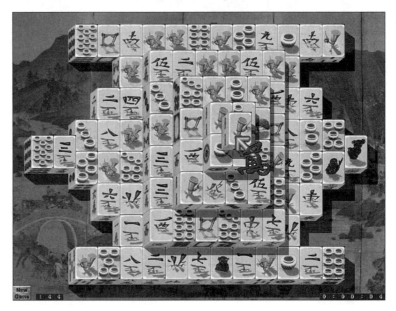

FIGURE 5.27
Easy to learn, difficult to master—Moraff's free mahjongg games are as addictive as they are attractive.

The goal is to clear the screen entirely, but it's not as easy as it seems—there are some tactics involved as there is more than one match per tile design and players have to be cautious not to render tiles underneath inaccessible.

Variations on this family-friendly game are also available free, including Moraff's MarbleJongg, Moraff's RingJongg, and Moraff's ArtJongg.

AMERICA'S ARMY

Designed by the U.S. Army, the goal of America's Army (www. americasarmy.com) is to provide civilians with a realistic perspective of military life. Two games in one, America's Army boasts a 3D action title where players strap into the boots of soldiers engaged in battle, as well as a role-playing game involving goals that must be accomplished to advance to officer status (see Figure 5.28).

FIGURE 5.28
Who said you can't get something for nothing? America's Army is one of the hottest action games around, and it's completely free—as long as you join the army. Just kidding.

America's Army, which is recommended for players 13 years of age or older (because of graphic violence), can be played solo or online in a number of cooperative team-based missions. File size is a whopping 640MB, but well worth it.

CHRYSLER WORLD TOURS GOLF

Desktop golfers can take a swing at this free downloadable game featuring two 18-hole courses: Myrtle Beach (a compilation of Tidewater, Blackmoor, Wild Wing Plantation, and Myrtlewood) and the Wildwood fantasy course. Players can indulge in this addictive diversion alone, but the real thrill is to join one of the many online tournaments to compete against up to three other virtual golfers (see Figure 5.29).

FIGURE 5.29
Hit the back nine with this free golf game—especially on those gorgeous days when you're stuck in a stinkin' cubicle.

This Chrysler World Tours (www.worldtoursonline.net) game features attractive graphics, online prize events, and a realistic swing simulation engine. Suitable for players of all ages.

DINK SMALLWOOD

Dink Smallwood (www.rtsoft.com) is a Zelda-esque fantasy adventure/role-playing game about a teenage farmer who goes from feeding pigs to saving the world as he learns to master both might and magic. Okay, so the story isn't anything to write home about, but the dozens of locations, characters, and side-quests makes this a must-have for those gamers on a mega-tight budget.

The game's graphics are inspiring for a freeware game, resembling the popular game Diablo, but with many more outdoor levels, including towns, an ice castle, and even the pits of hell itself (see Figure 5.30).

FIGURE 5.30
Don't let its silly name turn you off—Dink Smallwood is a blast to play. Slacking has never been this much fun.

Expect between 15 and 20 hours of play here, but most impressive is the fact Dink Smallwood players can also download 200 or so free MODs (modifications) for seemingly endless gameplay or create their own worlds using the free level editor.

A CHAT WITH THE "DON" OF SLACKING

You've read about Don's Boss! Page (www.donsbosspage.com) throughout this lengthy chapter—the man is the godfather of the high-tech slacking revolution. A book such as this would be remiss without a chat with the "Don" himself. Don Pavlish is a self-professed "web marketing guru" from Cleveland, Ohio, who started this popular web destination for those slackers.

Saltzman: Okay, Don, let's start with the basics. What is Don's Boss! Page? And what can you find here?

Pavlish: Don's Boss! Page is a website for slacking employees who are surfing the web from their workplace. The site brings up a realistic looking spreadsheet screen that fools your boss into thinking you're hard at work. The site also features "hard at work" sound effects to convince co-workers you're being productive behind your cubicle walls—while you're actually taking a nap or the afternoon off. There's also tips and tricks on how to surf the web at work without being caught, fun e-cards, and a floating panic button that keeps you protected during all your workplace web surfing.

Saltzman: So, the site gets traffic from serious slackers.

Pavlish: Indeed. The site is for workers who need to hide their illicit surfing from busybody bosses. It also attracts a lot of attention from bosses themselves, who are often upset with the site's negative contribution to workplace productivity.

Saltzman: We love it. How and when did you come up with the idea for it?

Pavlish: I created Don's Boss! Page in 1996, when workplaces were just beginning to provide Internet access to employees. The idea came from video games played on home computers of the 1980s, many of which featured a "boss button" keystroke command that brought up a fake spreadsheet.

Saltzman: Has Don's Boss! Page received any awards and accolades?

Pavlish: Yes, many. We've been written about on the front page of the *New York Times* and we've been in *USA Today*. We've also won a Geek Site of the Day award. It's great, and to think the site hasn't been updated in a long while. Visitors to the site, by the way, can read more about the many other awards and accolades we've received.

Saltzman: Have you done any broadcast media interviews?

Pavlish: Oh yes, including chats on NPR.

Saltzman: No kidding. That's great. Has anyone called in?

Pavlish: You bet. What I love about some of the radio chats I've done is that bosses will call in angry. That's always fun. They say, "You're helping employees slack off," but my response is that the site was meant to have fun. But getting bosses upset is always amusing. I mean, if a boss can't tell if an employee is slacking, then I'm not sure how good they are as a boss. I've also done some TV interviews, too.

Saltzman: What kind of traffic do you see at the site today? Or since it launched?

Pavlish: We average about 3000 hits a day, but of course we see major spikes whenever there's a newspaper article or radio appearance. Since '96, I've estimated that we get about one million visitors a year, so that's about eight million since we launched or thereabouts.

Saltzman: Wowza. Congratulations. If a half of one percent of those people buy this book, I'd be ecstatic (ahem). But I digress. Okay, so why do we slack? And is it wrong?

Pavlish: When it comes to web surfing on company time, we all have different vices. Some of us want to know sports scores, others like to gamble, some like to play computer games, or maybe you're into day trading. Or it may be to get stuff done such as holiday shopping, banking, or researching an illness for a relative. I say it's all harmless if you get your work done. The web is this tremendous resource for people and we're surfing for personal reasons at work because work is consuming more of our lives these days.

Saltzman: Tell me about it.

Pavlish: People are expected to work though lunch and more hours per week, or they're asked to stay late or come in weekends or take work home with them. And then the boss says, "Here's your cell phone so we can reach you anytime."

So I don't think there's anything wrong with [web surfing] since you're probably using the Internet for work already. What's wrong with that? Actually, when an employee uses the Net to order a gift for their kid, you're saving the employee a half-day off who would have to go and buy it or do their banking, and so on. You can argue that letting employees surf at work helps people balance work and their personal life. Again, the bottom line is that if they get their work done, it's all good. There are some limits, though, such as going to porn sites at work is a bad idea.

Saltzman: Oh, but I'm sure people have been caught by surfing to these naughty sites at work. Do you have any funny stories about people using your website and getting caught?

Pavlish: Every once in a while I receive email messages from people who used my sound effects such as typing—but don't know how to turn it off! I usually don't write back to them.

Saltzman: Oh that's cruel.

Pavlish: [Laughs] Well, some people are not very good with computers.

Saltzman: Anyone ever get fired by using the tools at your site such as the panic button or sound effects?

Pavlish: I hope not. I dunno, maybe they're now living in poverty and don't have email so I wouldn't know!

Saltzman: Ouch!

Pavlish: I sleep better at night not knowing about this. [Laughs] I know I've had students who have been caught in class for slacking at my site. One teacher caught on after a while—they're usually smarter than bosses. Actually, I've had the request to create a student version of Don's Boss! Page.

Saltzman: Good idea. Do you have any advice for slackers?

Pavlish: Become friendly with the IT department. Because I've heard of this happening before—upper management needs to cut jobs so they turn to the IT people and ask them to pull up logs of how many hours people are surfing on the Net. You know, to find an excuse to let them go and make an example out of them. The power of God is invested in the IT department. They are the intermediary between you and the boss, so you better be nice to them!

Saltzman: Any other advice?

Pavlish: Face the monitor away from the door and watch out for reflective surfaces behind you on the wall, such as a college diploma, because that could also show what's on your PC screen.

Saltzman: Good one. Yep, this is in our chapter on "non-tech" slacker tips.

Pavlish: Great! Here's another one: It's always important to maintain a very serious look on your face—look frustrated. Do things such as squint your eyes when you're surfing the Net because we don't realize how relaxed we look. You might even be kicking back with a smile on your face, which will give it away. You've got to check yourself. Besides, if you look upset, no one is going to bother you anyway.

Saltzman: Thanks, Don. Keep up the great work!

Pavlish: Thank you.

MORE SLACKING HELPS AND HINTS...

- Think you can only slack with high-tech gadgets? Be a corporate slacker and get away with it—the old-fashioned way. From George Costanza's advice to "look angry" to the ol' coat-on-the-back-of-the-chair trick.

- Want to gain respect among your co-workers (and help pass the time)? Discover all the best ways to play tech-related pranks on unsuspecting victims at the office.

- All the slacks you've gotten so far in this book not enough to satisfy? Discover the finest websites that feature online games, hilarious video clips and animations, web blogs, printable resignation letters, excuses for being late to work, and much more.

...SO WHAT ARE YOU WAITING FOR, GET SLACKING!

Chapter 6

Office Shenanigans

Tips and Practical Jokes for Surviving Another Day at the Office

• • • • •

W ell, we've covered quite a bit of tomfoolery in this book—from email and instant messaging tweaks to remote PC programs and other computer tricks, to how to use your favorite portable gadgets to slack the day away.

But guess what—we're not done just yet.

Disgruntled employees are always in need of reasons to stick it to the man, so this chapter offers even more delicious little schemes—ones that would even plant a smile on Dilbert's humble face.

First we take a look at some terrific practical jokes to play on your co-workers—especially tricks you can install on their PCs. After all, doesn't that know-it-all temp chick deserve it? Or how about that brown-nosing employee you just want to trip every time he saunters by your cubicle (you know the one, right)? I highlight a dozen or so PC-related programs that do everything from make it impossible to click on the Windows Start key to one that looks like you're unin-stalling all your programs to one that turns your mouse pointer into a hand that gives you the finger!

Then I profile more than a dozen exceptional websites you need to visit. Many of them offer ways to slack such as time-wasting games, video clips, terrific jokes, and Top 10 lists, while others let you vent by sharing stories about how mean your boss is.

Finally, I end this book with a handful of ways to make it look like you're working hard when you're not—without a PC or portable high-tech gadget in sight. What's this, you ask?

Don't Get Caught

If you haven't figured this one out already, here's a good way to read this book at the office without the boss catching wind of the title. Peel off a hardcover sleeve from, say, a business productivity book, and then wrap it around the *White Collar Slacker's Handbook*—and be sure to pick one that best fits this size. To be extra sure it's secure, take a little bit of clear tape and stick it to the inside flaps so it doesn't blow off while you stroll down the hallway to the cafeteria! Oh, you're so sneaky.

Okay, so the subtitle for this book is "Tech Tricks to Fool Your Boss," but because this guide is all about breaking (or at least bending) the rules, I take a page from that philosophy and drop in some info on non-tech tricks to fool your boss. Some are as old as the office itself. So kick back, enjoy, and soak it all in.

UNLEASH THE PRACTICAL JOKER IN YOU

If *The Apprentice* has taught us anything (other than all the money in the world doesn't guarantee a good haircut), it's that corporate culture can be cruel. It's a merciless, dog-eat-dog world out there—so why shouldn't you add a little levity to the office?

Arguably the best way to do so is to pick a victim, and then unleash a practical joke on him or her. For maximum enjoyment, get a few co-workers in on it and pick someone you really don't care for (and of course, make sure they're not a good sport!).

This part of Chapter 6 looks at slew of naughty—yet completely harm-less—programs to covertly install on your target's PC before she returns to her cubicle. When she sits back down and grabs hold of her mouse—watch out!

Unless otherwise specified, most of the following programs are free to download and use, and they all work with Windows 95 and higher.

Make Your Co-Worker Avoid His Start Button

Called Avoid, this straightforward joke program makes the Start button on the Windows operating system impossible to click! Watch as your co-worker tries to click it to launch a program. When the mouse cursor scrolls over the Start button, the button disappears and pops up elsewhere on the screen. When he tries to click it again, it bounces somewhere else. Take a picture of the puzzled or frustrated look on his face before telling him how to fix it (move the mouse to the top-left corner of the screen to turn it off). Download it for free at the main RJL Software Entertainment page at www.rjlsoftware.com/software/entertainment (see Figure 6.1). (©RJL Software Incorporated)

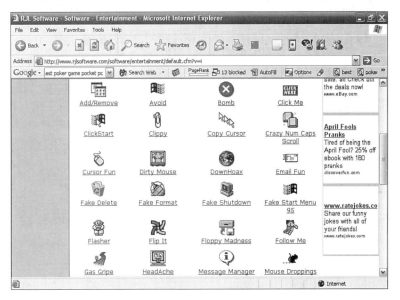

FIGURE 6.1
You can download more than 35 individual computer pranks free at the awesome RJL Software website. Simply click on the desired icon to read a description of the program and to learn how to successfully close the application (so your co-worker doesn't totally freak out). Click the link to download it.

Install Random Burper for a Full Range of Disgusting Noises

How embarrassing would it be for your boss or co-workers to hear a loud burp emanate from your cubicle every minute? This is precisely what Random Burper is all about. Secretly install this program on a PC (with speakers), and then wait for funny (and sometimes disgusting) variations to come out of the PC every 60 seconds. Listen long enough and you might even hear some flatulence. The program even turns the Windows volume up to its maximum and then returns back to normal once deactivated. Genius. (Random Burper©, RJL Software Incorporated; www.rjlsoftware.com/software/entertainment)

Start Moving, More Fun with the Start Button

Similar to Avoid is Start Moving, a tiny program that—as the name suggests—causes the Start button to move across the taskbar at the bottom of the screen. After double-clicking the downloaded file to install it, jokesters can even preset the speed and direction of the Start button's travels. Interestingly, even when it's on the move, the Start button still works so you can launch programs! (Start Moving ©1998 Lior Ostrowsky; www.leeos.com)

The Shocking Mouse Delivers a Jolt to Its User

Okay, this one is downright merciless. Remember those classic buzzer rings you can wear in your palm and when you shake someone's hand: ZAP! Well, the Shocking Mouse works on the same principle, but it's a PC mouse that delivers a minor shock to whomever touches it. Sounds harmless to us but the disclaimer on the website mentions: "This funny computer prank is not intended for children or adults with pacemakers or heart conditions!" (Shocking Mouse, $9.89; www.prankplace.com). An ideal way to pull off this prank is to tell a co-worker the boss finally upgraded all the mice in the office so she won't be suspicious. Or, you can ask someone to use your PC for a moment (for example, covertly call from another desk and ask her to look up a phone number on your PC for you). Then, make sure you have a clear line of sight when she sits down at your cubicle and grabs the mouse!

Cook Up Some Great Discussions for Break Time at StrangeReports.com

Give your co-workers a surprise they won't soon forget—this fun and free tool provided by StrangeReports.com lets you select a phony news story (police warrants, nose picker's society, missed lotto deadline, or toilet paper thief) and then asks that you type the victim's name and any other information that might be requested. Click on Submit Query, and then make sure your co-worker sees this new website with the fake news report, or print it out and make photocopies for the break room bulletin board (see Figure 6.2)! (StrangeReports.com)

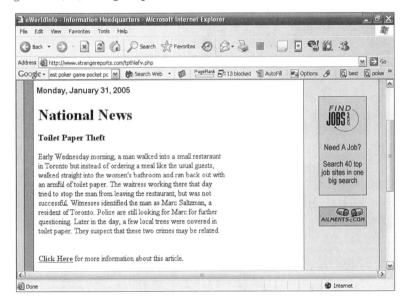

FIGURE 6.2
Oh, Marc, how could you? Imagine the look on your co-worker's face when he sees his name in this phony news article.

Give Your Co-Worker Hours of Frustration with Slippery Mouse

Want to drive your co-workers buggy? Install the free Slippery Mouse on their laptops or desktop computers and watch them try to take control over their mouse. This joke program makes this easy task a near impossible one as it seemingly turns your screen into a sheet of ice, sending the mouse cursor whizzing by uncontrollably. Once you think they've had enough, tell them you can turn this off by clicking on the tab on the taskbar at the bottom of the screen that says Slippery Mouse (yes, you'll be able to click it!). (Slippery Mouse ©RJL Software Incorporated; www. rjlsoftware.com/software/entertainment)

Noisy Keyboard Speaks for Itself

Noisy Keyboard installs various sound effects onto a computer so that when the unsuspecting victim presses a button on her keyboard, it plays a .wav audio file! Seven .wav files are included in this package, such as *boing!* and an old typewriter click (plus you can also import your own audio files). Installers can choose to assign sound effects to all the keys or just the spacebar, Enter key, four arrows, and so forth. (Noisy Keyboard ©1998 Lior Ostrowsky; www.leeos.com)

Win-Error and the Blue Screen of Death

Win-Error is a small program that simulates familiar Windows error messages, be it the "blue screen of death" or the various "illegal operation" error warnings. In order for this to work, PCs also need the free Visual Basic Runtime Module (if unsure, check the hard drive for this file: VBRUN300.DLL), which can also be downloaded from this site. A document is included with the download to explain how to install and run the program. Win-Error is free to try, $5 to buy. (Win-Error ©1997 KitSOFT™; www.pcworld.com/downloads)

Watch Your Step—Mouse Droppings Alert!

This silly prank causes your co-worker's mouse to leave little black mouse droppings all over the screen! By default, it excretes between one and four, er, turd pellets every three seconds, but you can configure the frequency to suit your fancy. When your co-worker has had enough, tell her to point the mouse in the upper-left corner of the screen and she'll see a splash screen with the message, "You have been pranked!" (Mouse Droppings ©RJL Software Incorporated; www.rjlsoftware.com/software/entertainment)

Email Fun on the Run

Ooh, this one is naughty, so save it for when you really need a laugh. Email this program, Email Fun, to co-workers and tell them it's a work-related document, so they must open it. When they do, it shows a fake email message on the computer screen, complete with the familiar To:, From:, Subject:, and message window. But what happens next is what will make their blood boil—the program automatically types an email to everyone in their address books and pretends to send the message (even if they try to click the X to close it)! (Email Fun ©RJL Software Incorporated; www.rjlsoftware.com/software/entertainment)

Add/Remove Programs Prank

Add/Remove is a clever piece of software that makes it look like it is uninstalling all the computer's programs. It resembles the familiar Add/Remove feature built into Windows and actually lists all the programs installed on that particular PC (see Figure 6.3). When the unsuspecting victim tries to close the application in a panic before more harm is done, nothing appears to work. When the prank is finished, a close button appears—he can click it to end the torture. But don't worry—when this fake Add/Remove program is finished, the victim sees a screen that assures him it was a joke and nothing was in fact removed from the computer. Whew! (Add/Remove ©RJL Software Incorporated; www.rjlsoftware.com/software/entertainment)

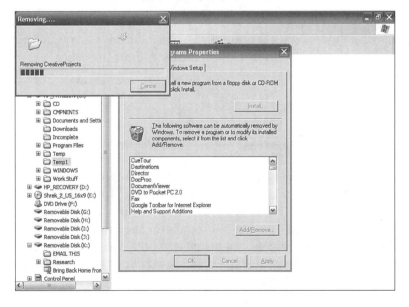

FIGURE 6.3
Imagine the panic on your co-worker's face when he or she sees all of his or her familiar computer programs apparently being deleted off the hard drive.

GIVE 'EM THE FINGER

Perhaps I've saved the best PC prank for last. When installed on a co-worker's Windows-based computer, The Finger causes the mouse cursor to quickly change to a small hand with the middle finger extended, and then switches back to the normal arrow once again. The default setting toggles this cursor to the middle finger every five seconds, but jokesters can change the frequency as desired. To stop this joke, push the mouse cursor to the top-left corner of the screen. (The Finger ©RJL Software Incorporated; www.rjlsoftware.com/software/entertainment)

SLACKING WEBSITES YOU SHOULDN'T MISS

In Chapter 5, I spoke with Don Pavlish of Don's Boss! Page (www.donsbosspage.com), who created a resourceful website for those who want to slack undetected.

But there are many other worthy websites to visit that can help you get through those rough days at the office. You know, when it feels like 4 p.m. and it's only 9:39 a.m.?

The following are a handful of fun cyberspace destinations to help during those times when you need a mental vacation from the office.

Disclaimer: Some of these websites contain adult themes, language, or imagery.

THE SCOTSMAN (WWW.SCOTSMAN.COM)

What better way to start off this section than by tipping our hat to the wonderfully written article for The Scotsman newspaper called "Is slacking the only way to survive the office?" by chief feature writer, Gillian Glover (at the main page, type "slacker" to search for the article). Be sure to read the "Slacker Commandments," near the end of the article. For example, number 7 is "Pretend to be a smoker—that way you get more paid time out of the office." Great idea!

KillSomeTime.com (www.killsometime.com)

If you find yourself twirling pens at your desk out of sheer boredom, visit KillSomeTime.com to help, well, kill some time. This site houses dozens of hilarious video clips (be sure to check out the infamously funny "Having a Bad Day?" movie), amusing pictures, celebrity mug shots, jokes and crank calls, Flash games and cartoons, and a KillSomeTime blog, to name a few sections.

IShouldBeWorking.com (www.ishouldbeworking.com)

From loafing tips and original cartoons to panic buttons (also seen in Chapter 5) and an "Office Survival" contest that seems to spoof *The Apprentice,* IShouldBeWorking.com has a ton of things to see and do for when you're lounging in your cubicle (see Figure 6.4). Be sure to try out the "Loafing Fun Greeting Cards" you can email to friends, such as an invitation to a "liquid lunch" and another that says "Let's Take a Day Off!" Sounds good to me.

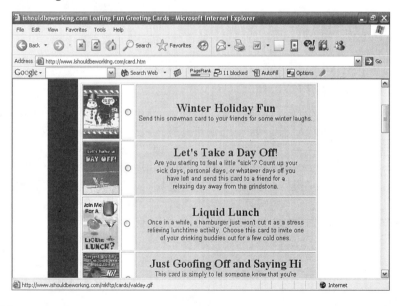

FIGURE 6.4
Having a bad day? Select one of these customizable e-cards to send to a friend or co-worker. Each one is catered to those who need a break away from the office (who doesn't?).

Bored At Work
(www.boredatwork.com)

Consider Bored At Work a springboard to hundreds of interesting websites, articles, animations, and games. Highlights include an article on "Understanding Your Employees' Hangover Level" and the hilarious "10 Worst Album Covers of All Time." There are so many web links to explore here (with warnings if they contain sound or music so you can turn your speakers down) that this bookmark-must will keep you entertained for years.

IWorkWithFools.com
(www.iworkwithfools.com)

"To show the world what a complete bunch of morons we all work with" is the first of 10 mission statements posted at IWorkWithFools.com, a site that lets you anonymously rant about idiotic co-workers and bosses. Submit a story, read a story, sign up for a newsletter, or partake in the "Fool Poll" with questions such as "How many fools are in your office place?" Great fun.

Recruiters Network "Call in Sick" Excuses
(www.recruitersnetwork.com/jokes/
callinsick.htm)

Read more than a dozen humorous reasons for not making it into work at this website hosted by the Recruiters Network. Examples include "If it is all the same to you I won't be coming in to work. The voices told me to clean all the guns today," or "When I got up this morning I took two Ex-Lax in addition to my Prozac. I can't get off the john, but I feel good about it." When all else fails, you might want to try this one: "I can't come in to work today because I'll be stalking my previous boss, who fired me for not showing up for work. Okay?" Badum-bum.

Office Diversions
(www.officediversions.com)

Subtitled "The Productivity Reduction Discovery Center," this fun website will keep you busy with its many sections, such as games, puzzles, articles, office jokes, and a section that lets you watch the clock hit 5 o'clock in different time zones (what a tease!). One of the funniest sections is "1,001 Office Diversions," including pranks such as switching the M and N keys on a co-worker's computer keyboard (it might take them a while to figure out what's wrong) or to change the mouse to left-handed in the Windows Control Panel!

SLACKER'S GUILD (WWW.SLACKERSGUILD.COM)

"What do you want to do half-assed today?" asks this humorous website that posts hundreds of discussions on topics ranging from how to get free stuff online, to relationship advice, to work-related musings from around the globe. Polls, related links, blog entries, forums, and contests round off this smart site. Be sure to visit the "Hall of Fame" section to read the most visited stories, the most active authors, the most active submitters, and the most popular poll topics.

THAT WAS FUNNY (WWW.THATWASFUNNY.COM)

This joke site has hundreds of categorized jokes to read when you're bored to tears. But I chose this site for its clever "14 Best Excuses If You Get Caught Sleeping At Your Desk." Favorites include "They told me at the blood bank this might happen," "This is just a 15 minute power-nap like they raved about in the last time-management course you sent me to," and "Whew! Guess I left the top off the liquid paper." Type "excuses" in the search window to read the full list.

CHRISTIAN'S & SCOTT'S INTERACTIVE TOP TEN LIST (WWW.CSITTL.COM)

Dozens of humorous "top ten" lists are here for your reading pleasure. My favorite is the "Top Ten Excuses for Being Late to Work," compiled in 1996 from various submissions, but it still holds up today. Type "late" in the search window to find the full list. Silly examples of excuses include "My arm got stuck in the blood pressure machine at K-Mart" and "I'm not late! I'm early for tomorrow," as well as "I was at a punctuality seminar." Ahem. (© 1995-2005, Scott Atwood and Christian Shelton)

WORKING STIFF "STRESS-O-METER" (WWW.WEBLAB.ORG/WORKINGSTIFF/STRESSOMETER)

Had enough? To see how much stress you're really under, fill out this interactive survey designed to measure the amount of stress you're experiencing in your workplace. Simply use the mouse to answer each of the multiple questions and the program will spit out a conclusion for you. An example of a question is, "Is everyone telling you to do something different? Does it seem like you have more than one boss and that it's unclear who you should listen to?" Answer one of the following: Hardly ever; Sometimes, but not often; Frequently; or Way too friggin' much.

DOWNLOAD.COM (WWW.DOWNLOAD.COM)

Arguably one of the largest file repositories on the Internet is Download.com, with its thousands of free downloads, all divided into sections and subsections (such as Games, and then Action/Arcade, or Music, and then Pop, and so on). All the downloadable freeware, shareware, and demo files contain a brief synopsis of the file, its size, supporting operating system, and more. You can spend a year at this site and never see the same thing twice! Hope you've invested in a large hard drive...

BBC LANCASHIRE—OFFICE FUN (WWW.BBC.CO.UK/LANCASHIRE)

Fans of the hit BBC comedy *The Office* should get a kick out of this website that offers everything from office dares and excuses for getting out of work to humorous printable certificates and the best ways for getting fired. Text and audio interviews with some of the series' cast members all add to the fun. You can even submit your own funny stories and pictures from your office.

IQUIT (WWW.IQUIT.ORG)

Had it with your snooty boss who looks down his nose at you? Tired of parking your dirty Honda Civic beside his shiny new Mercedes-Benz? If you must quit, you might as well do it in style. Such is the idea behind iQuit.org, a home to free resignation letters. According to this clever website, hundreds of thousands of people around the world have used their letter templates to quit their jobs since 1999. Send these by email or print them out for a more formal resignation.

Here's a particularly nasty one, entitled the "I Hate This Job, And You!" letter:

> Dear [Recipient's name]:
>
> Yesterday I woke up and realized that this is the worst career experience I've ever had. Therefore, I'm officially notifying you of my resignation from [company name]. My last day will be today.
>
> This company has many problems. [insert problems here]
>
> On top of that, I can't stand to work for you any longer. You, alone, have been a constant source of pain and suffering for me ever since I started this job. I can't understand how you made it this far in the professional community.
>
> Today is a great day for me. I will never have to see, hear, or listen to you ever again. Goodbye, and good-riddance!
>
> Warmest Regards,
>
> [Your Signature]

Ouch!

Also be sure to check out the UK-based I-resign.com (www.i-resign.com), with its discussion forum, printable resignation letter, guides to resigning, and a collection of "world famous" funny resignation letters.

No PC? No Gadgets? No Worries! (Re)Introducing the Classics

Although it goes against the grain of this book, there are plenty of non-tech office tips and tricks to pull off that make it look like you're working harder than you are.

Yep, a few timeless tricks might still do the trick in the 21st century. What do you have to lose?

Some have even been glorified in sitcoms such as NBC's *Seinfeld* and BBC's *The Office*, or flicks such as the hilariously underrated *Office Space*.

So let's kick it "old skool" for a bit.

Ye Old "Chair Cape"

An oldie but a goodie is to secretly leave a second jacket, coat, or blazer at work so when you need to step out early for the day to meet an old college buddy who blew into town, you simply throw the article of clothing over your chair before you leave. This means, of course, that you've only stepped out for a few moments to the casual passerby.

Naturally, you can't keep the coat over your chair all the time or no one will notice the change. So, if it's in your office, keep it behind the door. Cubicle squatters can keep it tucked in a drawer for when you really need it.

You can also change the location of the jacket from time to time. Why not throw it on your desk as if you just ran down to the restroom? You can lay it over your PC's monitor, too.

Trick the Boss

If you're lucky enough to sit in an office, be sure to angle your PC monitor in such a way that no one can see what you're doing. Just make sure nothing behind you, such as a college diploma, is reflecting that game of Windows Solitaire back to the boss. Cubicle users may opt for one of those old monitor screen covers so no one can see what's on your screen unless they're directly in front of it (check out www.fellowes.com).

Look Busy, Stupid

It's an age-old trick, but it works: You can never look too busy. Sure, pulling this off is a fine art that can take years to perfect.

The idea is that the busier you look, people will not only think you're the hardest working person at the company but your co-workers will also tend to leave you alone if they need help with something.

If you have a chair in your cubicle or office, another great way to get co-workers to leave you alone is to always keep a stack of books on them!

Imagine yourself scurrying down the office hallway, weaving in between cubicles, with an armful of manila folders and papers under your arm. Drop the occasional CD-ROM or diskette from time to time, stop to pick it up (and mumble something under your breath), and then continue going wherever you were headed. When you're at your desk, have a minimum of two phones on your ears at all times. Better yet, wear a headset phone—even when you're not on a call. From time to time, stand up, look like you're in a call by saying "uh huh" and glancing at the ceiling. Little do your boss or your co-workers know you're shopping on eBay.

Another tip is to carry boatloads of stuff home with you at night—books, papers, laptop computer, memos, day-timer—thus giving the false impression that you work longer hours than you do.

Oh yes, and leave the office later than everyone else. It doesn't matter if you've slipped the latest issue of *Esquire* magazine inside of a kiss-ass book such as *101 Tips to Becoming a Better Employee*. As long as the boss notices you're still there when he or she leaves, you've gained some brownie points. Granted, this advice is contradicted in the movie *Office Space*, where a hapless office drone avoids being seen by his manipulative boss at 5 o'clock—especially on Fridays—because he always stops by his cubicle to ask him to come in on weekends.

LOOK ANNOYED

Seinfeld's George Costanza pointed out that if you look impatient or irritated, people in the office will leave you alone.

Always look like you're pissed off about something. Or confused and perplexed. After all, if someone is approaching you with an issue and they see that you're already having a bad day, they may just pull a 180 and go and talk to "Julie the Temp" instead.

BE MESSY!

Some slacking experts say a messy desk is better than a clean one because it shows you've got a million things on the go. That is, to the observer, you're so freakin' busy with your tremendous workload that the last thing you have time for is desk aesthetics. Another way to look at it is that a clean desk means you have nothing to do but to alphabetically organize your desk top.

Volume matters, so pile up papers, books, folders, manuals, computer mice, CD-ROMs, and so forth. When someone asks for a document, always pull it out from the middle of the pile.

DON'T TOUCH THAT DIAL

While you're at it, screen your calls. Never pick up the phone unless you know it's your supervisor or boss calling. Instead, let your voice mail get it. Your co-workers aren't calling to give you anything other than a headache. You just know they want you to do something for them (especially that weasel in sales...you know the one I'm talking about, right?).

When somoene leaves you a voice mail message, call them back during the lunch hour so you can avoid them like the plague. It also looks like you're conscientiously working during your lunch break.

Come In to Work Early

One McDonald's (www. mcdonalds.com) television commercial from the summer of '04 shows a guy who races into work to get there early (naturally, he first picks up a breakfast to go from McDonald's). When his boss

Don't Get Caught

Another tip: If your co-worker is asking you to do something you really don't want to do (or if you really don't have time for it), ask him a follow-up question about it on his voice mail. If you delay the work with follow-up questions, he might just end up doing it himself, or he might ask some other lackey to do it for him. Try something like "Hey Jeff, can you please clarify what you had in mind?" or "Mike, I can do this for you but it needs to be after Thursday when I'm finished this project for the big man. You cool with that?" Sneaky, eh?

arrives at the office and sees he's not the first one there, he smiles and nods to the keen, committed employee. Little does the boss know the guy was only anxious to continue playing a computer game.

What can you learn from this TV commercial? Other than breakfast at McDonald's is yummy (although Morgan Spurlock from the *Super Size Me* documentary might disagree!), this employee looked like a diligent worker in his boss's eyes even though he came in early to catch up on a PC game. Great idea.

Another series of commercials is solely devoted to slacking. The Bud Light folks in Canada started a fun campaign called the "Bud Light Institute" (www.budlightinstitute.ca) that is solely dedicated to "providing solutions for men who strive to spend more time hanging out with friends and maybe having a beer."

One TV commercial shows a guy's desk with a steaming cup of coffee at all hours of the day. The employee is nowhere to be found but it doesn't matter as it seems he just left to do something. Does this guy ever stop working? Well, we later find out this is a fake cup of coffee that forever steams as if it was just poured. Nevertheless, his boss shakes his head in amazement at this tireless worker.

Index

Symbols

A

E

F

G

J - K

Q - R

S

T – U – V

Great Que and Sams books to read instead of working!

More great Que and Sams titles to read when you should be working!

iPod and iTunes Starter Kit
Tim Robertson
0-7897-3278-5
$34.99 US

Treo Essentials
Michael Morrison
0-7897-3328-5
$24.99 US

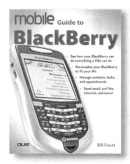

Mobile Guide to BlackBerry
Bill Foust
0-7897-3343-9
$24.99 US

Canning Spam: You've Got Mail (That You Don't Want)
Jeremy Poteet
0-672-32639-6
$29.99 US

Special Edition Using Microsoft Windows XP Professional, 3rd Edition
Robert Cowart,
Brian Knittel
0-7897-3280-7
$49.99 US

Special Edition Using Microsoft Office Outlook 2003
Patricia Cardoza
0-7897-2956-3
$39.99 US

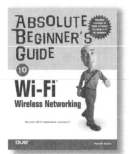

Absolute Beginner's Guide to Wi-Fi Wireless Networking
Harold Davis
0-7897-3115-0
$18.95 US

www.quepublishing.com

SAMS
www.samspublishing.com